30 German Short Stories for Complete Beginners

Grow Your German Vocabulary by Reading and Listening to Short Stories

For more products by Frédéric BIBARD, visit

https://mydailygerman.com

TABLE OF CONTENTS

INTRODUCTION

Everybody loves stories. I'm sure you do, too. So how would you like to learn German with the help of very short stories? It's fun and easy!

Most students who learn German as a second language say they are having the most trouble with the following issues:

- Lack of vocabulary
- Difficulty in picking up grammar structures, and
- Hesitation in speaking German because of (1) pronunciation troubles or (2) listening comprehension problems.

This collection of 30 very short stories will help you solve those challenges. At only 300 words per story, this book is created for complete beginners with little to no previous experience in learning German.

Learn new vocabulary

The stories in this book are written using the most useful German words. After each story, you will find a list of vocabulary used in the story together with its German translation. There is no need to reach for a dictionary each time you encounter words you don't understand, and you will quickly learn new words as you go along.

Easily grasp German sentence structures

Written with a good mix of descriptive sentences and simple dialogue, the stories will introduce you to different types of sentence structures. This way, you'll be able to naturally pick up German grammar structures as you read the stories.

Practice your listening comprehension

To be able to speak German well, you need to expose your ears to a lot of spoken German. You can do that by listening to the free audio narration of the stories. Listen to the words out loud and compare them to the written stories. Read along to the narration. Copy the correct pronunciation and practice the inflections. With enough practice, you will soon be able to get over your hesitations in speaking German.

Learning German as a second language can be a scary task. But with these short stories, you can make it as fun and as easy as possible. Before you know it, you have already learned hundreds of new German words, exposed yourself to a variety of sentence structures, and listened to enough spoken German that your pronunciation will improve greatly.

So go ahead. Start reading and have some fun!

Best of luck!

My Daily German Team

IMPORTANT: Please check at the end of the book how you can download the audio. (Page 134)

Der Wecker ist für 07:00 gestellt, aber ich wache früh auf. Es ist 06:30. Ich bin aufgeregt und zur gleichen Zeit nervös.

The alarm is set for 07:00 but I wake up early. It is 6:30. I am excited and nervous at the same time.

Es ist Montag und heute ist der Tag, an dem ich meine neue Arbeit beginne.

It's Monday and today is the day I start my new job.

Ich stehe auf und nehme eine Dusche. Dann mache ich Frühstück. Ich bin nicht hungrig, aber ich trinke einen Kaffee und esse eine Banane. Ich mache mir selbst ein Sandwich für mein Mittag.

I get up and take a shower. Then I have breakfast. I am not hungry but drink some coffee and eat a banana. I make myself a sandwich for my lunch.

Ich gehe, um mich anzuziehen. Ich wähle einen smarten Anzug und eine Bluse. Ich sehe in den Spiegel. Ich denke, dass ich zu formal aussehe und ändere meine Meinung. Ich finde ein dunkel gefärbtes Kleid und eine passende Jacke und fühle mich viel komfortabler.

I go to get dressed. I choose a smart suit and blouse. I look in the mirror. I think I look too formal and change my mind. I find a dark coloured dress and matching jacket and feel much more comfortable.

Ich putze meine Zähne und trage etwas Make-Up auf.

I clean my teeth and put on some make-up.

Ich finde meine Autoschlüssel, überprüfe dann die Zeit und realisiere, dass ich sehr früh dran bin. Es ist 07:15 und ich beginne um 08:30 zu arbeiten.

I find my car keys and then check the time, and realise that I am very early. It is 7:15 and I start work at 08:30!

Ich entschließe dennoch zu gehen, da ich nicht weiß, wie der Verkehr um diese Zeit ist. Ich sage auf Wiedersehen zu Peter und Henry.

I decide to leave anyway as I don't know what the traffic is like at this time. I say goodbye to Peter and Henry.

Ich komme in einer guten Zeit, um 08:00 herum, an, parke mein Auto am Parkplatz und gehe durch die Tür von meinem neuen Büro. Ich benötige 3 Minuten, um dorthin zu gehen.

I arrive in good time, at about 08:00, park my car in the car park, and make my way to the door of my new office. It takes me 3 minutes to walk there.

Ich klopfe an der Tür. Meine Chefin, Janet, kommt zur Türe und lässt mich rein.

I knock on the door. My boss, Janet, comes to the door and lets me in.

Einige Personen arbeiten bereits und sie stellt mich meinen neuen Kollegen vor. Sie sagt, „Das ist Sarah. Sie ist die neue Büroleiterin".

Some people are already working and she introduces me to my new colleagues. She says, "This is Sarah. She's the new office manager".

Jeder ist sehr freundlich und sie sagen „Hallo", „Hi" und „Nett, Sie kennenzulernen", als ich ihnen vorgestellt werde.

Everybody is very friendly and they say "Hello", "Hi" and "Pleased to meet you," as I am introduced to them.

Janet zeigt mir, wo die Toiletten und die Küche sind, dann zeigt sie mir meinen Schreibtisch. Ich setze mich hin und beginne zu arbeiten.

Janet shows me where the toilets are, and the kitchen, then she shows me to my desk. I sit down to start work.

Ich habe eine Menge zu lernen, und der Vormittag vergeht sehr schnell.

I have a lot to learn and the morning passes very quickly.

Bald ist es Mittagszeit. Ich entschließe mich, in die Küche zu gehen, um mein Sandwich zu essen und Kaffee zu machen.

Before long, it is lunchtime. I decide to go to the kitchen to eat my sandwich and make some coffee.

Ich öffne meine Tasche und sehe hinein.

I open my bag and I look inside.

Ich leere meine Tasche aus. Ich schaue alles an, dass ich herausgenommen habe. Wo ist das Sandwich?

I empty out my bag. I look at everything I have taken out. Where is the sandwich?

Ich schaue nochmal. Doch da ist kein Sandwich.

I look again. Still there is no sandwich.

Dann eben bloß Kaffee zum Mittag.

Just coffee for lunch then.

Difficult Words

1- Sich anziehen – To get dressed

2- Ein smarter Anzug – A smart suit

3- Eine Bluse – A blouse

4- Frühstück – Breakfast

5- Make-up auftragen – Put on make-up

6- Verkehr – Traffic/ circulation

7- Chef (m)/Chefin (f) – Boss

8- Büroleiter (m)/Büroleiterin (f) – Office manager

9- Die Küche – The kitchen

10- Ich setze mich hin – I sit down

11- Mittagessen – Lunch

12- Ich nahm – I took

13- Nett, Sie kennenzulernen – Nice to meet you

14- Arbeiten – To work

15- Eine passende Jacke – A matching jacket

Zusammenfassung der Geschichte:

Aufgeregt und nervös ist Sarah bereit, heute ihre neue Arbeit anzutreten. Sie nimmt sich Zeit, sich gut auf den ersten Tag vorzubereiten und kommt früh an, aber etwas verläuft nicht so wie geplant.

Summary of the Story:

Feeling excited and nervous, Sarah is ready to start her new job today. She takes time to prepare well for her first day and arrives early, but something is not going as planned.

Quiz:

1) Was isst Sarah zu Mittag?

    a) Ein Sandwich und einen Kaffee.

    b) Eine Banane und einen Kaffee.

    c) Nur einen Kaffee.

What does Sarah eat for lunch?

    a) A sandwich and a coffee.

    b) A banana and a coffee.

    c) Only a coffee.

2) Sarah ist:

    a) Die neue Büroleiterin.

    b) Ersatz für Janet.

    c) Die neue Chefin.

Sarah is :

    a) The new office manager.

    b) Janet's new replacement.

    c) The new boss.

3) Janet ist:

    a) Sarahs Kollegin.

    b) Eine Freundin von Sarah.

    c) Sarahs Chefin.

Janet is:

    a) The colleague of Sarah.

    b) The friend of Sarah.

    c) The boss of Sarah.

ANSWERS:

    1) C

    2) A

    3) C

Ich sitze mit meinem Kaffee in der Personalküche und schaue auf meine Nachrichten am Handy. Jede Menge Freunde senden mir „Viel Glück" -Nachrichten für meinen ersten Tag mit meiner neuen Arbeit.

I sit with my coffee in the staff kitchen and look at my phone messages. Lots of friends are sending me "good luck" messages for my first day in my new job.

Meine Kollegen fangen an, alleine und zu zweit in die Küche zu kommen und alle sind freundlich und sagen hallo. Sie kommen herüber, dort wo ich sitze und schließen sich mir mit ihren Mittagessen an.

My colleagues start to come into the kitchen in ones and twos and they are all friendly and say hello. They come over to where I am sitting and join me with their lunch.

Sie stellen mir Fragen über mich, wo ich lebe, ob ich in einer Beziehung bin, welche anderen Arbeiten ich gemacht habe, und so weiter.

They ask me questions about myself, where I live, if I'm in a relationship, what other jobs I have done, and so on.

So, hier sind die Antworten:

So, here are the answers:

Mein Name ist Sarah und ich bin 38 Jahre alt.

My name is Sarah and I am 38 years old.

Ich lebe in Slimbridge, welches ein kleines Dorf, etwa 25 Kilometer vom Büro entfernt, ist. Dort gibt es in etwa 150 Häuser, ein Pub, ein Postamt, einen Zeitungshändler und ein Lebensmittelgeschäft. Die Kirche ist im Zentrum des Dorfes und dort ist ein Park mit Fußballfeldern und Tennisanlagen, wohin alle Kinder spielen gehen.

I live in Slimbridge which is a small village about 25 kms away from the office. There are about 150 houses there, a pub, a post office and newsagent, and a grocery store. The church is at the centre of the village and there is a park with football pitches and tennis courts where all the children go to play.

Ich bin seit 11 Jahren mit Peter, einem Lehrer, verheiratet und wir haben einen Sohn, welcher 8 Jahre alt ist. Henry ist voller Energie und möchte immer etwas tun. Wir alle lieben es, Sport zu treiben und Henry

ist im Fußballteam des Dorfes. Er spielt samstags morgens Spiele und Peter und ich gehen mit, um zu helfen, wenn wir können.

I have been married to Peter, a teacher, for 11 years and we have a son, Henry, who is 8 years old. Henry is full of energy and wants to be busy. We all like to do sport and Henry is in the village football team. He plays matches on a Saturday morning, and Peter and I go along to help when we can.

Mein Ehemann und ich spielen Badminton in den Wintermonaten und Tennis im Sommer. So oft wie wir können, gehen wir mit Henry schwimmen.

My husband and I play badminton in the winter months and tennis during the summer. We go swimming with Henry as often as we can.

Alle meine Arbeiten beinhalteten Administration und fanden in einem Büro statt Ich bin gut in Papierarbeit und sehr organisiert. Ich arbeitete fünf Jahre lang für eine Bank, eine Abteilung verwaltend und hörte dort auf, als Henry geboren wurde.

All of my jobs have involved administration and working in an office. I am good at paperwork and am very organised. I worked for a bank for five years, managing a department, and left there when Henry was born.

So nun kennen sie mich besser.

So now they know me better.

Die Mittagspause endet und wir alle gehen plaudernd und lächelnd zurück zum Büro.

The lunch break ends and we all go back to the office chatting and smiling.

Difficult Words

1- Senden mir – Sending me

2- Schließen sich mir an – Join me

3- Viel Glück – Good luck

4- Ich lebe – I live

5- Arbeiten – Jobs

6- Mein Name ist – My name is

7- Lebensmittelgeschäft – Grocery store

8- Kirche – Church

9- spielen – To play

10-Lehrer (m)/ Lehrerin (f) – Teacher

11- Sohn – Son

12-Winter – Winter

13-Sommer – Summer

14-Büro – Office

15-Papierarbeit – Paperwork

Zusammenfassung der Geschichte:

Sarah setzt ihren ersten Tag bei der Arbeit fort und knüpft Kontakte mit ihren Kollegen, die eine Menge Fragen über sie stellen.

Summary of the Story:

Sarah continues her first day at work and socializes with her colleagues who ask her a lot of questions about her.

Quiz:

1) In dem Dorf, in dem Sarah lebt, gibt es kein(e):
   a) Kneipe
   b) Lebensmittelgeschäft
   c) Krankenhaus

In the village where Sarah lives, there is not:
   a) A bar
   b) A grocerie store
   c) A hospital

2) Sarah und Peter sind wie viele Jahre verheiratet?
   a) 8 Jahre
   b) 11 Jahre
   c) 25 Jahre

Sarah and Peter have been married for how many years?
   a) 8 years
   b) 11 years
   c) 25 years

3) Im Sommer spielen Sarah und ihr Ehemann:
   a) Badminton
   b) Fußball
   c) Tennis

During the summer, Sarah and her husband play:
   a) Badminton
   b) Football
   c) Tennis

ANSWERS:
   1) C
   2) B
   3) C

Der Arbeitstag geht dem Ende zu und ich denke an meine Reise nach Hause. Es ist 17:30.

The working day comes to an end and I think about my journey home. It is 17:30.

Ich warte darauf, dass jeder geht, dann nehme ich meine Tasche und hole die Büroschlüssel heraus. Ich bin, da ich nun die Büroleiterin bin, dafür verantwortlich, das Büro abzuschließen und es jeden Morgen zu öffnen.

I wait for everybody to leave then pick up my bag and take out the office keys. I am responsible for locking the office, and opening it each morning, now that I am the office manager. So, I need to arrive first in the morning.

Es gibt da einen Sicherheitsalarm einzustellen, sowie die Fenster zu überprüfen. Ich muss sicherstellen, dass die Computer ausgeschaltet sind. Ich mache alles und benötige dafür etwa 15 Minuten. Ich bin sicher, morgen werde ich schneller sein.

There is a security alarm to set as well as windows to check. And I must make sure the computers have been switched off. I do all of that and it takes me about 15 minutes. I'm sure I will be quicker tomorrow.

Ich fahre in meinem Auto davon und komme in einen Stau. Es kostet mich länger als eine Stunde, um die 25 Kilometer nach Hause zu fahren. Ich komme um 18:45 daheim an.

I drive away in my car and join a traffic jam. It takes me more than an hour to drive the 25 kms home. I get home at 18:45.

Ich dachte beim langsamen Fahren daran, mit dem Zug oder Bus zu reisen, anstelle des Autos.

I spend the slow driving thinking about travelling by train or by bus instead of by car.

Es gibt da zwei Optionen:

These are my options:

- **Die Bushaltestelle ist nur 5 Minuten Gehzeit von meinem Haus entfernt, und die Busse fahren einmal pro Stunde um Viertel nach. Die Reise dauert eine volle Stunde. Wenn ich an der Bushaltestelle rausgehe, habe ich einen Gehweg von 15 Minuten vor mir. Wenn ich den Bus um 07:15 nehme, verlasse ich das Haus um 07:10, 5 Minuten früher als diesen Morgen. Ich denke, ich werde beim Büro um 08:30 ankommen. Das ist knapp, da ich um 08:30 zu arbeiten beginne.**

- The bus stop is only 5 minutes' walk from my house and the buses run once per hour at a quarter past. The journey takes a full hour. When I get off at the bus station, I have a 15-minute walk ahead of me. If I take the bus at 07:15, I will leave the house by 07:10, 5 minutes earlier than this morning. I think I will arrive at the office at 08:30. That's tight as I start work at 08:30.

- **Zur Zugstation ist eine 10 Minuten-Fahrt von zu Hause und es gibt wenig Parkplätze dort. Die Züge gehen jede halbe Stunde, um 5 und 35 Minuten nach jeder vollen Stunde. Die Reise dauert 25 Minuten. Die Gehzeit von der Station zu meinem Büro beträgt 10 Minuten. Um den Zug zu nehmen, muss ich um 07:15 das Haus verlassen – um sicher zu sein, dass ich parken kann und zur Plattform komme – für den Zug um 07:35. Ich steige um 08:00 aus dem Zug und kann um 08:10 im Büro sein.**

- The train station is a 10-minute drive from home and there is little parking there. The trains run every half hour at 5 and 35 minutes past each hour. The journey takes 25 minutes. The walk from the station to my office is 10 minutes. To take the train, I need to leave home at 07:15 – to be sure to be able to park, and to get to the platform – for the train at 07:35. I get off the train at 08:00 and can be at the office for 08:10.

Als ich nach Hause komme, überprüfe ich die Kosten für das Reisen mit dem Bus und mit dem Zug. Ich vergleiche sie mit den Kosten für das Reisen mit dem Auto – Kosten für den Parkplatz ebenso, wie für den Sprit.

When I get home, I check the cost of travelling by bus and travelling by train. I compare the costs with travelling by car - paying for the car park as well as the cost of the petrol.

Unabhängig der Kosten beschließe ich, dass Bequemlichkeit wichtiger ist, und ich werde weiterhin mit dem Auto reisen.

Regardless of the cost, I decide that convenience is more important and I will continue to travel by car.

Difficult Words

1- Haus – House

2- Ich warte – I wait

3- Ich nehme – I take/ I pick up

4- Schlüssel – Keys

5- Erst – First

6- Abschließen – Closing/ locking

7- Fenster – Windows

8- Ich überprüfe – I check

9- Computer – Computers

10- Abgeschaltet – Switched off

11- Stau – Traffic jam

12- Eine Reise – A travel

13- Parkplatz – Parking

14- parken – To park

15- Kosten – Costs

Zusammenfassung der Geschichte:

Sarah beendet ihren ersten Arbeitstag und macht sich auf den Heimweg. Auf dem Weg wird sie von Verkehr aufgehalten, und sie erwägt andere Möglichkeiten zur Arbeit zu kommen.

Summary of the Story:

Sarah ends her first day at work and returns home. Along the way, she is slowed down by traffic and starts considering her other options for getting to work.

Quiz:

1) Warum entschließt sich Sarah, weiterhin mit dem Auto zur Arbeit zu fahren?

   a) Weil das Auto günstiger als der Zug ist.

   b) Weil das Auto bequemer ist.

   c) Weil sie mit dem Auto Zeit sparen kann.

Why did Sarah choose to continue to drive her car to work?

   a) Because the car is cheaper than the train.

   b) Because the car is more convenient.

   c) Because she can save time by taking the car

2) Wie lange dauert es, bis Sarah zu Hause ankommt?

   a) Mehr als eine Stunde

   b) 25 Minuten

   c) 45 Minuten

How long does it take for Sarah to arrive home?

   a) More than an hour

   b) 25 minutes

   c) 45 minutes

2) Um welche Uhrzeit würde Sarah im Büro ankommen, wenn sie den Zug nähme?

   a) 8 Uhr

   b) 07:35 Uhr

   c) 08:10 Uhr

What time would Sarah arrive at the office if she'll take the train?

   a) 8h

   b) 7h35

   c) 8h10

ANSWERS:

   1) B

   2) A

   3) C

Es gibt eine Menge zu bedenken, wenn Sie planen, in den Urlaub zu fahren.

There is a lot to think about when you are planning a holiday.

Als erstes müssen Sie sich entscheiden, wohin es geht. Haben Sie ein Ziel im Kopf? Vielleicht haben Sie eins, vielleicht nicht.

Firstly, you need to decide where to go. Do you have a destination in mind? You may have, but you may not.

Vielleicht möchten Sie einen Aktivurlaub machen, oder vielleicht einen Urlaub, um eine andere Kultur oder Sprache zu lernen. Oder Sie möchten an einem Pool liegen oder an einem Strand und nichts tun, außer für die Zeit ihres Urlaubs zu entspannen. Oder vielleicht eine Kombination von allen 3.

You may want to go on an activity holiday, or perhaps a holiday to learn about a different culture or language, or you may want to lie by a pool or on a beach and do nothing but relax for the duration of your holiday. Or perhaps a combination of all 3.

Sie müssen entscheiden, wie Sie ihre Zeit verbringen wollen.

You have to decide on how you want to spend your time.

Und Sie müssen sich ebenso entscheiden, mit wem Sie gehen, speziell dann, wenn Sie und Ihr Reisepartner nicht übereinstimmen darin, wohin gehen und was tun.

And you may also have to decide who to go with, especially if you and your travel party can't agree on where you're going or what you're doing.

In der Realität sind Ihre Optionen nahezu endlos, aber so sind auch die zu treffenden Entscheidungen. Das Internet ermöglicht, eine breite Palette an Ideen, Zielen und Aktivitäten zu berücksichtigen und abenteuerlicher zu sein, als es jemals möglich war.

In reality, your options are almost endless, but so are the decisions to be made. The Internet enables you to consider a vast range of ideas, destinations and activities, and to be more adventurous than it has ever been possible to be.

Hier sind die zu nehmenden Schritte:

So here are the steps to take:

1. Entscheiden Sie sich, mit wem sie verreisen wollen.

1. Decide who you are going to go away with.

2. Vereinbaren Sie Ihr Budget.

2. Agree your budget.

3. Vereinbaren Sie ein Datum, an dem Sie beide (oder alle) verreisen können.

3. Agree dates when you are both (or all) able to get away.

4. Diskutieren Sie, wie Sie ihre Zeit fernab verbringen wollen – beschäftigt sein, aktiv sein, kultiviert sein, faul sein, oder etwas ganz anderes. Oder eine Kombination von alle dem. Falls Sie nicht bei allem übereinstimmen können, stimmen Sie vielleicht für einen Teil der Zeit einem „Machen Sie ihr eigenes Ding" zu.

4. Discuss how you want to spend your time away – being busy, being active, being cultured, being lazy, or being something else altogether. Or a combination of them all. If you can't agree on everything, perhaps agree to 'do your own thing' for some of the time.

5. Verbringen Sie etwas Zeit damit, darüber zu reden, wo Sie übernachten wollen: Camping? In einem Hotel oder einer Villa? Mit einer Familie? Unter den Sternen?

5. Spend a little time talking about where you want to stay: camping? In a hotel or villa? With a family? Under the stars?

6. Erwägen Sie, ob Sie den ganzen Urlaub selber planen wollen, oder ob Sie die Hilfe eines Reiseveranstalters in Anspruch nehmen.

6. Consider if you want to plan the entire holiday yourselves, or whether you welcome the help of a travel agent.

7. Beschließen Sie ihr Land, dann grenzen Sie es auf ihr tatsächliches Reiseziel oder Reiseziele ein und die Schlüsselaktivitäten.

7. Agree your country, then narrow it down to your actual destination or destinations, and the key activities.

Da Sie es nun soweit gebracht haben, denken wir daran, wie wir das eigentlich alles möglich machen.

Now that you've got this far, let's think about how we actually make this happen.

Difficult Words

1- Urlaub – Holiday
2- lernen – To learn
3- liegen – To lie
4- Pool – Pool
5- Strand – Beach
6- entspannen – Relax
7- Du möchtest – You want
8- Gehen – To go
9- Endlos – Endless
10-Abenteuerlustig – Adventurous
11- Faul – Lazy
12-Sterne – Stars
13-Hilfe – Help
14-Land – Country
15-Lass uns nachdenken – Let's think

Zusammenfassung der Geschichte:

Zu verreisen erfordert eine Menge Vorbereitung. Wichtiger noch, es erfordert, viele wichtige Entscheidungen zu treffen. Mit wem verreisen? Welche Art von Aktivitäten möchten Sie in ihrem Urlaub unternehmen? Was ist ihr Budget? Diese Geschichte beschreibt die Schritte, wenn man einen Urlaub vorbereitet.

Summary of the Story:

Going on vacation requires a lot of preparation, but more importantly, it requires to take a lot of important decisions. Who to go with? What kind of activity do you want to do during your vacation? What is your budget? This story describes the steps on what to take when preparing a vacation.

Quiz:

1) Welche der folgenden Optionen ist kein Vorteil, wenn man das Internet benutzt, um eine Reise zu planen?

    a) Es ermöglicht, eine riesige Spannbreite an Ideen, Reisezielen und Aktivitäten in Betracht zu ziehen.

    b) Es ermöglicht, das Unmögliche möglich zu machen.

    c) Es ermöglicht, abenteuerlustiger als jemals möglich zu sein.

Which of the following options is not an advantage of using the internet to plan your vacations?

    a) It enables you to consider a vast range of ideas, destinations and activities.

    b) It allows you to make the impossible possible.

    c) It enables you to be more adventurous than it has ever been possible to be.

2) Wenn Sie und ihr Partner sich im Hinblick auf mögliche Aktivitäten während des Urlaubs nicht einigen können, geht man am Besten wie folgt vor:

    a) Kompromisse eingehen; unternehmen Sie Aktivitäten, die ihr Partner machen möchte, auch wenn Sie selber diese nicht machen möchten.

    b) Den Partner wechseln und Freunde finden, die exakt das tun möchten, was Sie tun möchten.

    c) Sich einigen, dass jeder für eine Weile seinen eigenen Kram macht.

If you and your companion are unable to agree on the activities to do during your vacations, it is best to:

    a) Make compromises; do activities that your companion wants to do even if you don't want to.

    b) Change partners and find a friend who wants to do exactly what you want to do.

    c) Agree to do your own stuff for a while.

3) Was ist der letzte Schritt, den man machen muss, wenn man eine Reise plant?

   a) Das Budget festlegen.

   b) Entscheiden, ob man den ganzen Urlaub selber planen oder die Hilfe eines Reisebüros in Anspruch nehmen möchte.

   c) Das Land festlegen, das genaue Reiseziel oder die genauen Reiseziele bestimmen und die Schlüsselaktivitäten.

What is the last step in taking action when planning a trip?

   a) Agree your budget.

   b) Consider if you want to plan the entire holiday yourselves, or whether you welcome the help of a travel agent.

   c) Agree your country, then narrow it down to your actual destination or destinations, and the key activities.

ANSWERS:

   1) B

   2) C

   3) C

Wir wissen, dass es eine Menge zu bedenken gibt, wenn Sie in den Urlaub fahren. Es kann stressig sein, aber wenn Sie gut organisiert sind, ist es das nicht.

We know there is a lot to think about when you're going on holiday. It can be stressful, but it isn't if you're well-organised.

Bis jetzt wissen Sie, mit wem Sie gehen und wann. Sie wissen, wie viel Sie ausgeben wollen oder ausgeben können, wo Sie übernachten wollen und was Sie machen wollen, während Sie weg sind. Ebenso kennen Sie ihre Reiseziele, welches ohne Frage, die wichtigste, zu treffende Entscheidung ist.

By now, you know who you're going with, and when. You know how much you want to spend or are able to spend, where you want to stay and what you want to do while you're away. You also know your destination, which is arguably the most important decision to be made.

Nehmen wir an, dass Sie dies selbst arrangieren und buchen, ohne die Hilfe eines Reisebüros. Sie werden sehen, dass die Kosten so niedriger sind, aber das Risiko manches Mal höher ist, daher ist es keine einfache Entscheidung.

Let's assume that you're arranging and booking this yourself, without the help of a travel agent. You will find the costs are lower this way, but the risks are sometimes higher, so it isn't be an easy decision.

Die folgenden Tipps und Schritte werden Dinge einfacher machen:

The following advice and steps will make things easier:

1) **Wählen Sie eine gute Fluggesellschaft, in die Sie Vertrauen haben. Überprüfen Sie die Verfügbarkeit von Flügen für den Zeitraum, in dem Sie reisen wollen.**

1) Choose a good airline that you have confidence in. Check availability of flights for the dates you want to travel.

2) **Suchen Sie nach Plätzen zum Übernachten. Überprüfen Sie die Verfügbarkeit von Unterkünften für den Zeitraum, in dem Sie weg sein wollen. Denken Sie daran, was inkludiert ist, und was extra ist.**

2) Look up places to stay. Check availability of accommodation for the dates you want to be away. Think about what is included and what is extra.

3) Überprüfen Sie, welche Aktivitäten mit denen übereinstimmen, die Sie machen wollen, während Sie unterwegs sind.

3) Check out which activities match those you want to do while you are away.

4) Wenn alles stimmt, überprüfen Sie ihre Zeiträume noch einmal, und dann buchen Sie die Flüge. Sie haben vermutlich mehr als einen Platz zum Übernachten, aber es gibt vermutlich nur einen Flug, der ihnen passt, also buchen Sie zuerst die Flüge.

4) If everything matches up, check your dates again, then book your flights. You probably have more than one place to stay but there is probably only one flight that suits you, so book your flights first.

5) Dann überprüfen Sie ihre Zeiträume noch einmal und buchen Ihre Unterkunft.

5) Then check your dates again, and book your accommodation.

6) Und nun denken Sie daran, ihre Aktivitäten zu buchen. Bevor Sie das tun, entscheiden Sie sich, welche für Sie die Wichtigsten sind. Sehen Sie sich die Versicherung an, die jeder einzelne Aktivitätenanbieter anbietet und stellen Sie sicher, dass dieser Ihre Sicherheit ernst nimmt.

6) And now plan to book your activities. Before you do, decide which are the most important to you. Look at the insurance each activity provider offers and make sure they take your safety seriously.

7) Nun überprüfen Sie ihre Zeitangaben noch einmal, dann schreiten Sie voran und buchen Ihre Aktivitäten.

7) Now, check your dates again, then go ahead and book your activities.

8) Und schließlich nehmen Sie sich sofort eine Reiseversicherung. Stellen Sie sicher, dass diese Ihre Flüge, Unterkünfte, medizinische Versorgung und all Ihren Besitz abdeckt. Denken Sie daran, wie viel Sie ausgeben und beachten Sie, dass alles abgedeckt ist.

8) And finally, take out travel insurance straightaway. Make sure it covers you for your flights, accommodation, medical needs, and all your belongings. Think about how much you are spending and make sure everything is covered.

Bewahren Sie Ihre Belege an einem sicheren Platz auf.

With everything, keep your receipts in a safe place.

Und nun planen Sie einfach, Ihre Reise zu genießen, wann immer sie kommt.

And now, just plan to enjoy your trip, whenever it comes around.

Difficult Words

1- Stressig – Stressful

2- Organisiert – Organized

3- Ausgeben – To spend

4- Jetzt – Now

5- So / auf diese Weise – This way

6- Einfach – Easy

7- Fluggesellschaft – Airline

8- Flüge – Flights

9- Unterkunft – Accomodation

10- Bedürfnisse – Needs

11- Belege – Receipts

12- Sicherer Ort – Safe place

13- Genießen – Enjoy

14- Anbieter – Provider

15- Nachschlagen / Suchen – Look up

Zusammenfassung der Geschichte:

Nachdem Sie die wichtigsten Entscheidungen bei der Vorbereitung ihrer Reise getroffen haben, wie zum Beispiel die Person, mit der Sie verreisen, die Art der Unterkunft, in der Sie bleiben möchten und welches Budget vorliegt, ist es wichtig, gute Ratschläge und Schritte zu befolgen, um den Trip ohne die Hilfe eines Reisebüros zu organisieren.

Summary of the Story:

After having decided on the most important decisions to prepare your trip such as the destination, the person with whom to go with, the type of accommodation where you want to stay and the budget you have, it is important to follow several advice and steps to organize your trip without the help of a travel agent.

Quiz:

1) Was ist ein wichtiger Schritt, bevor man die Aktivitäten bucht?

a) Einen Blick auf die Versicherung werfen, die jeder Anbieter von Aktivitäten anbietet.

b) Die günstigste Aktivität auswählen.

c) Die am wenigsten gefährliche Aktivität auswählen.

What is the important step to take before booking the activities?

a) Look at the insurance each activity provider offers.

b) Choose the cheapest activity.

c) Choose the least dangerous activity.

2) Die Reiseversicherung sollte abdecken:

a) Nur die Flüge.

b) Medizinische Bedürfnisse.

c) Den gesamten Betrag, den Sie ausgeben.

Travel insurance must cover:

a) Flights only.

b) Medical needs.

c) The total amount of your spending.

3) Wenn alle Vorbereitungsschritte erledigt sind, was ist wichtig zu tun?

a) Entspannen und auf den Reisestart warten.

b) Die Belege an einem sicheren Ort verwahren.

c) Einen Plan B-Trip vorbereiten, für den Fall, dass die Flüge storniert werden.

Once all the preparation steps have been completed, what is important to do?

a) Relax and wait for the journey to begin.

b) Keep your receipts in a safe place.

c) Prepare a plan B trip in case your flights are canceled.

ANSWERS:

1) A

2) C

3) B

GESCHICHTE 6: ESSEN IM AUSLAND EINKAUFEN
STORY 6: FOOD SHOPPING ABROAD

Essen in einem fremden Land zu kaufen ist eine Freude und eine lernende Erfahrung. Es ermöglicht Ihnen, so viele kulturelle Unterschiede zu sehen und zu verstehen und vielleicht die unterschiedlichen Lebensweisen zu verstehen.

Shopping for food in a foreign country is a pleasure and a learning experience. It enables you to see and understand so many cultural differences and, perhaps, to understand the different way of life.

In kalten Ländern ist Essen oftmals schwer und voll von Kohlenhydraten, da die Menschen, die dort leben, zusätzlich Kalorien verbrennen müssen, um sich warm zu halten. Sie wählen Essen, das ihre Mägen füllt und von innen heraus wärmt und welches eine lange Zeit zum Kochen benötigt . Sie freuen sich, einen offenen Ofen oder ein Feuer brennen zu haben, wenn nötig, für Stunden, um ihr Essen durch zu kochen. Es ist eine zusätzliche Quelle von Wärme in einer kalten Klimazone. Oft enthalten Supermärkte bloß Essen, dass etwas fad aussieht. Es hat wenig Farbe, da es unter der Erde im Dunkeln wächst und wenig Sonne sieht. Daher kann es unappetitlich oder uninteressant aussehen. Es sieht wenig verlockend zum Essen aus, wird jedoch trotzdem gut schmecken.

In cold countries, food is often heavy and full of carbohydrates, as the people who live there need to burn extra calories to keep themselves warm. They choose foods that will fill their stomachs and warm them from the inside, and which may take a long time to cook. They are happy to have an oven on, or a fire burning, for hours if necessary, to cook their food thoroughly. It is an additional source of heat in a cold climate. Often, the supermarkets only contain food which looks a little boring. It has little colour as it's grown underground or in the dark, and sees little sun. It can therefore seem unappetising or uninteresting. It certainly looks less tempting to eat, but will still be tasty.

In wärmeren Ländern, auf der anderen Seite, bevorzugen Menschen oft, nicht zu viel zu kochen. Sie wollen nicht durch einen Ofen oder ein Feuer heizen, um ihr Zuhause noch wärmer zu machen und sie wollen kein heißes Essen in ihren Körper geben. Sie dürften einfaches Essen auswählen, dass am besten roh gegessen wird, also sind frische Früchte, Gemüse und Salate das, was oft gesehen wird, sowie Essen, dass beim Kochen wenig Zeit benötigt, um durchgekocht zu sein.

In warmer countries, on the other hand, people often prefer not to cook very much at all. They do not want the heat from an oven or fire to make their home even warmer, and they do not want to put hot food inside their body. They may choose simple food that is best eaten raw, so fresh fruit and vegetables, and salads, are often what is seen, as well as foods that, if cooked, take little time to cook through.

In den Märkten und Supermärkten in einem warmen Land werden Sie eine Reihe an bunten Früchten und Gemüse sehen, um Ihren Gaumen zu verführen, sowie eine große Auswahl an Kräutern. Die Sonne bringt die Farben an die verfügbaren Früchte. Es wird oft Essen geben, von dem Sie noch nie zuvor gehört oder es gesehen haben. Das wird oft einhergehend mit Fisch bemerkt, bei solchen, die bloß in lokalen Gewässern gefunden werden.

In the markets and supermarkets in a warm country, you will see an array of colourful fruit and vegetables to tempt your palette, as well as a big range of herbs. The sun brings colour to the foods available. There will often be foods you have never seen or heard of before. These will very often be seen alongside a variety of fish, some of which are only found in the local waters.

Machen Sie sich die Mühe, wenn Sie reisen, die lokale Nahrung zu essen und nehmen Sie die Kultur an, die Sie erfahren.

When you travel, make an effort to eat and enjoy the local foods and to embrace the culture you are experiencing.

Difficult Words

1- Kaufen – To buy/Shopping

2- Essen – Food

3- Fremd – Foreign

4- Lernen – Learning

5- Ofen – Oven

6- Verstehen – To understand

7- Kalt – Cold

8- Schwer – Heavy

9- Verbrennen – To burn

10- Magen – Stomach

11- Hitze – Heat

12- Unappetitlich – unappetizing

13- Wohlschmeckend – Tasty

14- Langweilig – Boring

15- Unter der Erde – Underground

Zusammenfassung der Geschichte:

In einem anderen Land Nahrungsmittel einzukaufen ist ein Vergnügen und eine Lernerfahrung in Bezug auf einen Aspekt der Kultur des besuchten Landes. Welcher Unterschied besteht zwischen Essen in kalten und Essen in wärmeren Ländern und warum? Diese Geschichte beantwortet diese Fragen.

Summary of the Story:

Shopping for food in a foreign country is a pleasure and a learning experience on an aspect of the culture of the country visited. What is the food difference between the cold countries and warm countries and why? This story answers these questions.

Quiz:

1) **Warum bevorzugen Menschen in warmen Ländern einfaches und rohes Essen?**

   a) **Weil sie nicht stundenlang kochen möchten.**

   b) **Weil sie nicht möchten, dass die Hitze des Herds ihr Zuhause noch mehr aufheizt.**

   c) **Weil sie nur Nahrungsmittel haben, die wenig Zeit brauchen, um zu garen.**

Why do people in warm countries prefer to eat simple and raw food?

   a) Because they don't like to cook for hours.

   b) Because they do not want the heat from an oven or fire to make their home even warmer.

   c) Because they only have foods that take little time to cook.

2) **Warum sind Früchte und Gemüsesorten auf Märkten in warmen Ländern farbenreich?**

   a) **Weil die Sonne ihnen Farbe bringt.**

   b) **Weil sie unter der Erde wachsen.**

   c) **Weil diese Nahrungsmittel mit einer Vielfalt an Fisch einhergehen.**

Why fruits and vegetables in markets of warm country are colorful?

   a) Because the sun brings colour to the food.

   b) Because these s grows underground.

   c) Because these foods are be seen alongside a variety of fish.

3) **Was ist die Empfehlung am Ende der Geschichte?**

   a) **Wenn man verreist, sollte man Essen mitnehmen, um seine Kultur zu teilen.**

   b) **Wenn man verreist, sollte man lokalen Fisch essen.**

   c) **Wenn man verreist, sollte man sich bemühen, einheimische Speisen zu essen und zu genießen.**

What is the recommendation at the end of this story?

  a) When you travel, bring food to share your culture.

  b) When you travel, eat the local fish.

  c) When you travel, make an effort to eat and enjoy the local foods.

ANSWERS:

  1) B

  2) A

  3) C

GESCHICHTE 7: EIN BESCHÄFTIGER TAG IN DEN FERIEN (1)
STORY 7: A BUSY DAY IN THE HOLIDAYS (1)

"Papa! Papa! Können wir schwimmen gehen?"

"Dad! Dad! Can we go swimming?".

„Es ist jetzt Zeit für das Bett. Wir können darüber am Morgen reden."

"It's time for bed now. We can talk about it in the morning."

Es sind Schulferien und da ich ein Lehrer bin, sehe ich nach meinem Sohn, Henry. Und nach dem Hund, Charlie. Henry ist 8 Jahre alt und voll mit Energie und will beschäftigt sein. Er will raus gehen und jeden Tag etwas machen, aber wir müssen auch einiges an Hausarbeiten machen.

It's the school holidays and, as I am teacher, I look after our son, Henry. And the dog, Charlie. Henry is 8 years old and full of energy, and wants to be busy. He wants to go out and do something every day but we need to do some jobs at home as well.

Er wacht jeden Tag früh auf, und heute ist es nicht anders. Er fragt sofort, ob wir schwimmen gehen können. Ich biete ihm einen Deal an.

He gets up early every day and today is no different. He asks immediately if we can go swimming. I offer him a deal.

„Wir können schwimmen gehen, wenn wir einige Arbeiten beendet haben. Wirst du mir helfen, die Aufgaben zu machen?"

"We can go swimming when we have finished some jobs. Will you help me to do the jobs?"

Es sieht mich an, noch unsicher, nervös darüber, was er machen müsse. Er antwortet nicht, also erkläre ich:

He looks at me, still unsure, nervous about what he might have to do. He doesn't answer so I explain:

„Wir müssen den Geschirrspüler entleeren, abwaschen, die Wäsche machen und staubsaugen. Was willst du machen?", frage ich ihn.

"We have to empty the dishwasher, wash up, put the washing on, and hoover. Which do you want to do?", I ask him.

Er sieht mich an, noch immer unsicher.

He looks at me again, still unsure.

Schließlich sagt er: „Kann ich stattdessen das Auto waschen?"

Eventually he says, "Can I wash the car instead?".

Ich denke sorgfältig über sein Angebot nach. Das Auto muss gereinigt werden, aber ich möchte nicht zu einfach nachgeben. Ich möchte ihm zu verstehen geben, dass es harte Arbeit zu machen gibt und er seine Belohnung verdienen muss.

I think carefully about what he is offering. The car does need cleaning but I don't want to give in too easily. I want him to understand that there is hard work to do and he has to earn his treats.

Ich erinnere mich, dass er einmal zuvor mein Auto wusch, aber ich war bei ihm. Dieses Mal muss er es alleine machen.

I remember that he washed my car once before, but I was with him. This time he needs to do it on his own.

Ich halte inne und laufe in der Küche umher, denkend. Er fragt mich noch einmal und noch einmal, „Bitte Papa, kann ich stattdessen das Auto waschen?".

I pause and wander around the kitchen, thinking. He asks me over and over, "Please Dad, can I wash the car instead?".

Nach einer angemessenen Pause gebe ich nach. Ich bringe ihn zur Garage, um den Eimer, den Schwamm und das Auto-Shampoo zu finden und überlasse es ihm.

After a reasonable pause, I give in. I take him to the garage to find the bucket, sponge and car shampoo, and leave him to it.

Ich mache mit meinen Arbeiten im Haus weiter, in Frieden und dem Radio lauschend und ich sehe nach ihm alle 15 Minuten. Ich sehe, er arbeitet hart und nimmt seine Arbeit ernst.

I carry on with my jobs in the house, in peace and listening to the radio, and I check on him every 15 minutes. I see he is working hard and taking his job seriously.

Er ist fertig und wirft den Schwamm in den Eimer hinein mit einem Ruf, „Papa, ich bin fertig," und ich gehe nach draußen, um seine Arbeit zu überprüfen.

He finishes and throws the sponge into the bucket with a shout of, "Dad, I've finished," and I go outside to check his work.

Ich bin erstaunt, wie sauber und glänzend das Auto nun ist und sage ihm, er ist ein beeindruckender Autoreiniger.

I am amazed at how clean and shiny my car is and tell him he is an amazing car cleaner.

Wir gehen zurück in das Haus und packen unsere Schwimmkleidung und gehen zum Schwimmbad.

We go back into the house and pack our swimming clothes, and head to the swimming pool.

Nach unserem Schwimmen sagt er, " Ich habe das wirklich genossen, Papa. Ich fühle mich wirklich so, als ob ich mir meine Belohnung verdient habe!".

After our swim, he says, "I really enjoyed that, Dad. I really feel as if I earned my treat!".

Und ich stimme ihm zu.

And I agree with him.

Difficult Words

1- Schwimmen – To swim

2- Bett – Bed

3- Lehrer (m)/Lehrerin (f) – Teacher

4- Hund – Dog

5- Ausgehen – To go out

6- Irgendetwas – Something

7- Deal – Deal

8- Unsicher – Unsure

9- Nervös – Nervous

10- Antworten – Answer

11- Geschirrspüler – Dishwasher

12- Abwaschen – Wash up

13- Staubsauger – Hoover

14- Sorgfältig – Carefully

15- Belohnung – Treats/Rewards

Zusammenfassung der Geschichte:

Es sind Schulferien, und Henry, ein 8-jähriges Energiebündel, möchte ständig ausgehen und etwas unternehmen, während sein Vater mit mehreren Tätigkeiten beschäftigt ist. Heute besteht Henry darauf, schwimmen zu gehen. Daher bietet ihm sein Vater einen Deal an.

Summary of the Story:

It's school holidays and Henry, an 8-year-old energy ball, always wants to go out and do activities while his father is busy with several tasks to do. Today, Henry insists on going for a swim, so the father offers him a deal.

Quiz:

1) Was ist eine der Pflichtaufgaben, die der Vater Henry anbietet?

    a) Den Hund füttern und mit ihm spazieren gehen.

    b) Den Abwasch machen.

    c) Sein Zimmer aufräumen.

What is one of the tasks that the father suggests Henry to do?

    a) To feed and walk the dog.

    b) To put the washing up.

    c) To clean his room.

2) Warum zögert Henrys Vater, dass er das Auto wäscht?

    a) Weil das Auto keine Wäsche benötigt.

    b) Weil er nicht sicher ist, dass er es alleine machen kann.

    c) Weil er ihm zu verstehen geben möchte, dass es harte Arbeiten zu erledigen gibt und er seine Belohnung verdienen muss.

Why did Henry's father hesitate that he washed the car?

    a) Because the car does not need cleaning.

    b) Because he is not sure if he can do it by his own.

    c) Because he wants him to understand that there is hard work to do and he has to earn his treats.

3) Am Ende der Geschichte ist Henry:

    a) Zufrieden, dass er hart gearbeitet und seine Belohnung verdient hat.

    b) Traurig, weil er nicht länger im Schwimmbad bleiben kann.

    c) Ängstlich, dass er erneut hat arbeiten muss, um eine Belohnung zu erhalten.

At the end of the story, Henry is:

    a) Happy to have worked hard and earned his treat.

    b) Sad to not be able to stay longer at the pool.

    c) Anxious to have to work again to earn a treat.

ANSWERS:

    1) B

    2) C

    3) A

GESCHICHTE 8: SCHOKOLADENKUCHEN
STORY 8: CHOCOLATE CAKE

Beim Backen von Kuchen denken Sie an Folgendes:

When baking cakes, remember the following:

- **Kuchen werden besser warm gegessen.**
- Cakes are better eaten warm.
- **An Heißen Speisen können Sie sich verbrennen, wenn Sie sie berühren.**
- Hot dishes can burn you if you touch them.
- **Sie müssen die Zutaten sorgfältig abmessen.**
- You must measure the ingredients carefully.
- **Es ist besser, sie zu genießen, solange sie frisch sind.**
- It is better to enjoy them while they are fresh.

Lassen Sie uns über einige wichtige Details nachdenken, wenn Sie einen Schokoladenkuchen machen.

Let's think about some important details when making a chocolate cake.

ZUTATEN:
  - **100 Gramm Mehl**
  - **100 Gramm Zucker**
  - **100 Gramm Butter**
  - **2 Eier**
  - **Schokolade – Echte Schokolade oder Pulver**

INGREDIENTS:
  - 100 grams of flour
  - 100 grams of sugar
  - 100 grams of butter
  - 2 eggs
  - Chocolate – real chocolate or powdered

Wenn Sie den Anweisungen sorgfältig folgen, wird es köstlich sein.

If you follow the instructions carefully, it will be delicious.

1) **Kaufen Sie alle Zutaten im Voraus und benutzen Sie diese, solange sie noch frisch sind.**

1) Buy all of the ingredients in advance and use them while they are still fresh.

2) **Messen Sie die Hauptzutaten ab – Eier, Mehl, Butter und Zucker – sehr sorgfältig und dann mischen Sie diese zusammen, bis die Masse glatt und cremig ist. Das wird 5 bis 10 Minuten dauern. Es ist einfacher, wenn die Butter bereits weich ist.**

2) Measure out the main ingredients - eggs, flour, butter and sugar - very carefully and then mix them together until the mixture is smooth and creamy. This may take 5 to 10 minutes. It is easier if the butter is already soft.

3) **Geben Sie die geschmolzene Schokolade hinzu, nachdem die Masse für 10 Minuten in einem Kühlschrank gekühlt hat. Wenn Sie echt Schokolade hinzugeben, schmelzen Sie sie behutsam und langsam. Falls Sie die Schokolade überhitzen, wird sie klumpig werden und Sie werden nicht in der Lage sein, sie zu benutzen. Wenn Sie bevorzugen, Schokoladen-Pulver, statt geschmolzener Schokolade hinzuzugeben, seien Sie sicher, dass es zuvor gesiebt wurde und dann geben Sie es langsam zur Kuchen-Masse hinzu.**

3) Add the melted chocolate when the mixture has cooled in the fridge for 10 minutes. If you add real chocolate, melt it very gently and slowly. If you overheat the chocolate, it will go lumpy and you will not be able to use it. If you prefer to add powdered chocolate instead of melted chocolate, make sure it is sieved first and then add it slowly to the cake mixture.

4) **Schalten Sie den Ofen an, so dass er genug aufwärmt, bis Sie soweit sind, die Masse zum Backen hinein zu geben und sodass der Kuchen gleichmäßig gebacken wird.**

4) Turn on the oven so that it is warm enough when you are ready to put the mixture in to cook, and so that the cake is cooked evenly.

5) **Giesen Sie die Masse in eine geölte Backform (oder 2 Backformen).**

5) Pour the mixture into a greased dish (or 2 dishes).

6) **Wenn die Speisen fertig sind, geben Sie diese in den Ofen. Für 20 Minuten backen lassen.**

6) When the dishes are ready, put them in the oven. Cook for 20 minutes.

7) **Wenn der Kuchen fertig ist, denken Sie daran, die Backform nicht mit ihren Händen zu berühren, wenn Sie sie aus dem Ofen nehmen, da sie zu heiß sein wird. Benutzen Sie einen Topfhandschuh.**

7) When the cake is ready, remember not to touch the baking dish with your hands when you take it out of the oven as it will be too hot. Use an oven glove.

8) Drehen Sie den Kuchen aus seiner Backform und lassen Sie ihn abkühlen.

8) Turn the cake out of its tin and leave to cool.

9) Sobald er abgekühlt ist, schneiden Sie eine Scheibe ab und genießen Sie.

9) Once cool, cut a slice and enjoy.

Difficult Words

1- Kuchen – Cakes

2- Abmessen – Measure

3- Frisch – Fresh

4- Machen – Making

5- Mehl – Flour

6- Zucker – Sugar

7- Butter – Butter

8- Ei – Egg

9- Mixen – Mix

10-Weich – Soft

11- Klumpig – Lumpy

12-Gesiebt – sieved

13-Langsam – Slowly

14-Gekocht – Cooked

15-Handschuh – Glove

Zusammenfassung der Geschichte:

Einen Schokoladenkuchen zu backen erfordert, dass man mehrere Schritte sorgfältig befolgt. Diese Geschichte erzählt, wie man einen köstlichen Schokoladenkuchen zubereitet und diesen sicher bäckt.

Summary of the Story:

Baking a chocolate cake requires following several steps very carefully. This story tells how to prepare a delicious chocolate cake and how to cook it safely.

Quiz:

1) Wie lange sollte der Kuchen backen?

    a) 5-10 Minuten

    b) 10 Minuten

    c) 20 Minuten

How long should the cake bake for?

    a) 5-10 minutes

    b) 10 minutes

    c) 20 minutes

2) Was ist der nächste Schritt, nachdem man den Kuchen aus dem Ofen genommen hat?

    a) Den Kuchen aus der Form nehmen und abkühlen lassen.

    b) Ein Stück abschneiden und genießen

    c) Kuchenglasur auftragen.

What is the next step after taking the cake out of the oven?

    a) To turn the cake out of its tin and leave to cool.

    b) To cut a slice and enjoy.

    c) To add the cake frosting.

3) Was passiert, wenn man die Schokolade überhitzt?

    a) Die Schokolade brennt an, und der Kuchen wird ein Brandaroma haben.

    b) Die Schokolade wird unbrauchbar, da sie zu cremig wird.

    c) Die Schokolade klumpt.

What happens if you overheat the chocolate?

    a) Chocolate will burn, and the cake will have a small burn flavor.

    b) Chocolate becomes unusable because it will become too creamy.

    c) Chocolate will go lumpy.

ANSWERS:

    1) C

    2) A

    3) C

GESCHICHTE 9: WIE MAN SCONES BACKT
STORY 9: HOW TO BAKE SCONES

Scones sind klassische, englische Teezeit-Leckerbissen und sie sind sehr einfach zu machen. Dieses Scones-Rezept ist auch einfach zu variieren, falls Sie einen anderen Geschmack oder eine andere Füllung versuchen wollen.

Scones are a classic English tea-time treat, and are very easy to make. This scone recipe is also easy to change if you want to try a different flavour or filling.

ZUTATEN:

- **225g mit Backpulver gemischtes Mehl**
- **Eine Prise Salz**
- **55g weiche Butter**
- **25g Streuzucker**
- **150ml Milch**
- **1Freilandei, geschlagen, zum lasieren (obwohl Sie alternativ ein bisschen Milch benutzen können)**

INGREDIENTS:

- 225g of self-raising flour
- a pinch of salt
- 55g of soft butter
- 25g of caster sugar
- 150ml of milk
- 1 free-range egg, beaten, to glaze (although you could, alternatively, use a little milk).

Zubereitung:

METHOD:

1) **Erhitzen Sie den Ofen auf 200°C.**

1) Heat the oven to 200°C.

2) **Fetten Sie das Backbleck leicht ein, oder geben Sie ein Stück fettdichtes Papier darauf.**

2) Lightly grease a baking sheet, or put a piece of greaseproof paper on it.

3) **Mischen Sie das Mehl mit dem Salz zusammen, reiben Sie danach die geweichte Butte unter.**

3) Mix together the flour and salt, then rub in the softened butter.

4) Rühren Sie den Zucker ein, Stück für Stück, und geben Sie danach die Milch dazu, um einen weichen Teig zu erzeugen.

4) Stir in the sugar, a little at a time, and then add the milk to make a soft dough.

5) Bearbeiten Sie die Masse gut mit Ihren Händen in einer Rührschüssel, geben Sie diese danach heraus, auf eine mehlige Oberfläche und kneten Sie sie nochmals leicht.

5) Work the mixture well with your hands in the mixing bowl, then turn it out onto a floured surface and knead it again lightly.

6) Streicheln Sie die Masse aus in eine grobe 2 cm dicke Form. Benutzen Sie einen 5cm Stecher, um runde/individuelle Scones zu machen und platzieren Sie diese auf einem Backblech.

6) Pat out the mixture into a round shape roughly 2cm thick. Use a 5cm cutter to make rounds / individual scones, and place them on the baking sheet.

7) Rühren Sie zusammen, was vom Teig übrig geblieben ist und wiederholen Sie Schritt 6. Machen Sie damit weiter, bis Sie die ganze Masse zum Machen von Scones verwendet haben.

7) Pull together what is left of the dough and repeat Step 6. Keep doing this until you have used all of the mixture to make scones.

8) Pinseln Sie die Oberseite der Scones mit dem geschlagenen Ei ein (oder der Milch). Schieben Sie das Backblech in den Ofen

8) Brush the tops of the scones with the beaten egg (or the milk). Put the baking sheet in the oven.

9) Backen Sie sie zwischen 12 und 15 Minuten, bis sie gut aufgegangen und auf der Oberfläche golden sind.

9) Bake for between 12 and 15 minutes until well risen and golden on the top.

10) Kühlen Sie die scones auf einem Gitterrost ab und servieren Sie sie mit Butter und einer guten Marmelade (Erdbeere passt sehr gut), oder vielleicht Schlagsahne, anstelle der Butter.

10) Cool on a wire rack and serve with butter and a good jam (strawberry works very well), or maybe some clotted cream instead of the butter.

Sie können das Rezept ändern, indem Sie getrocknete Früchte bei Schritt 4 hinzugeben. Sie können ebenso Gewürze hinzufügen, wie Muskatnuss oder Zimt.

You can change the recipe by adding dried fruit at Step 4. You can also add some spices such as nutmeg or cinnamon.

Sie können nach Käse (-schmeckende) Scones machen, indem Sie den Zucker weglassen und 100 Gramm geriebenen Käse hinzufügen. **Ein starker Käse, so wie Cheddar funktioniert am besten.**

You can make cheese (savoury) scones by leaving out the sugar and adding 100 grams of grated cheese. A strong cheese such as cheddar works best.

Genießen Sie!

Enjoy!

Difficult Words

1- Rezept – Recipe

2- Geschmack – Flavor

3- Füllung – Filling

4- Selbsttreibend – Self raising

5- Milch – Milk

6- Geschlagen – Beaten

7- Glasieren – To glaze

8- Backpapier – Baking sheet

9- Kneten – To knead

10-Marmelade – Jam

11- Mischung – Mixture

12-Gewürze – Spices

13-Käse – Cheese

14-Zimt – Cinnamon

15-Muskat – Nutmeg

Zusammenfassung der Geschichte:

Diese Geschichte beschreibt, wie man Scones backt, welche Zutaten man benötigt und welche Möglichkeiten man hat, um Scones in verschiedenen Geschmacksrichtungen zu erhalten.

Summary of the Story:

This story describes how to cook scones, its ingredients and the different options for obtaining scones with different flavors.

Quiz:

1) Welche Zutat kann man anstatt des Eis benutzen?

   a) Milch

   b) Puderzucker

   c) Weiche Butter

What ingredient can you use instead of the egg?

   a) Milk

   b) caster sugar

   c) Soft Butter

2) Wie lange müssen die Scones im Ofen backen?

   a) 8 bis 10 Minuten

   b) 12 bis 15 Minuten

   c) 20 Minuten, bis sie gut aufgegangen sind und oben eine goldige

What is the cooking time of the scones in the oven?

   a) 8 to 10 minutes

   b) 12 to 15 minutes

   c) 20 minutes, until well risen and golden on the top

3) Welche Zutat wird nicht für Scones empfohlen?

   a) Marmelade

   b) Streichrahm

   c) Schokolade

Which of these ingredients is not recommended to be used with scones?

   a) Jam

   b) Clotted cream

   c) Chocolate

ANSWERS:

   1) A

   2) B

   3) C

GESCHICHTE 10: INTERNET
STORY 10: INTERNET

Mit dem Beginn der modernen Technologie können Menschen heutzutage praktischer und bequemer das Leben genießen, als die ältere Generation.

With the advent of modern technology, people today can enjoy more convenient and comfortable lives compared to the older generations.

In diesem Informationszeitalter sind Suchmaschinen, wie Google, Safari und Bing unter allen die meist genutzten Computer-Applikationen, auf Grund ihres Komforts und Potentiales.

In this Information Age, search engines such as Google, Safari and Bing are amongst the most widely used computer applications because of their convenience and potential.

Mit nur einfachen Computer-Fähigkeiten können Menschen einfach Antworten für ihre Probleme finden, sowie zur gleichen Zeit ihre Neugier befriedigen.

With only basic computer skills, people can easily find answers to their problems at the same time as satisfying their curiosity.

Viele Studenten machen übermäßig oft Gebrauch von Suchmaschinen für akademische Zwecke. Sie vertrauen manchmal einzig auf Suchmaschinen für ihre Informationen und erforschen keine anderen Informationsquellen, wie Bücher zu lesen oder sich in Konversationen mi ihren Mitstudenten zu engagieren. Sie könnten leicht ihren Sinn für Neugierde verlieren.

Many students make excessive use of search engines for academic purposes. They sometimes rely solely on search engines for their information and do not explore other sources of information, such as reading books or engaging in conversations with their fellow students. They can easily lose their sense of curiosity.

Schlaue Studenten verbringen mehr Zeit darin, ihre Informationen aus der echten Welt zu erhalten, anstelle von öffentlichen, Online-Quellen und kommen so mit einzigartigeren, individuelleren und interessanteren Antworten daher.

Wise students spend more time gathering their information from the real world rather than public, online sources and so come up with more unique, individual, and interesting answers.

Computers und Technologie spielen eine maßgebliche Rolle im Leben von Menschen, aber sie können ebenso deren Privatsphäre beeinflussen.

Computers and technology do play a vital role in peoples' lives, but they can also affect their privacy.

Es ist für Kriminelle einfach, die Informationen einer Person zu sehen und das Risiko dafür ist größer, wenn eine Person nicht ernsthaft darüber nachdenkt, wie sie seinen/ihren Computer benutzt.

It is easy for criminals to see an individual's information and the risk of this is greater if an individual does not think seriously about how they use their computer.

Eingriff in die Privatsphäre mag im digitalen Zeitalter unausweichlich erscheinen, aber es sollte nicht sein. Es war einmal nahezu unmöglich, jemandens Bankdaten, Geburtstag, oder Sozialversicherungsnummer ausfindig zu machen, ohne dessen Genehmigung. Aber heute scheinen diese Details einfach zu finden zu sein.

Invasion of privacy may seem inevitable in this digital age, but it should not be. It used to be almost impossible to find out somebody's bank details, date of birth, or social security number, without their permission. But today, these details seem to be so easy to find out.

Seiten sozialer Netzwerke ermutigen Menschen offen über deren Privatleben zu sein und Informationen zu teilen, die nützlich für andere sind, die es für kriminelle oder bösartige Zwecke nutzen wollen.

Social networking sites encourage people to be open about their private lives and to share information that is useful to others who wish to use it for criminal or malicious purposes. People are naturally sociable and want to share their experiences, but doing so through the use of technology can cause them problems in their lives.

Personen können Kontrolle über ihre Leben haben und ein signifikanter Teil davon ist, wie sie ihre Computer und das Internet nutzen.

Individuals can take control of their lives and how they use their computer and the Internet is a significant part of this.

Difficult Words

1- Beginn – Advent
2- älter – Older
3- Suchmaschinen – Search engines
4- Bequemlichkeit – Convenience
5- Fähigkeiten – Skills
6- Studenten – Students
7- Kluge – Wises
8- Einzigartiges – Uniques
9- Digitalzeitalter – Digital age
10- Geburtsdatum – Date of birth
11- Erlaubnis – Permission
12- Soziale Netzwerkseiten – Social networking sites
13- Teilen – To share
14- Bankdaten – Bank détails
15- Sozialversicherungsnummer – Social security number

Zusammenfassung der Geschichte:

Das Internet hat die Welt der Technologie revolutioniert. Heute nutzen Menschen es aufgrund seines Nutzens und des Potenzials täglich. Sie können ein komfortableres Lebens als frühere Generationen genießen, aber das Internet hat auch negative Seiten, denen frühere Generationen nicht zum Opfer gefallen sind.

Summary of the Story:

Internet has revolutionized the world of technology. Now, people use it daily because of its convenience and potential. They can enjoy a more comfortable life than previous generations, but Internet also brings negative aspects to which previous generations could not have been victims.

Quiz:

1) **Welche dieser Konsequenzen wird nicht erwähnt, wenn Studenten sich zu akademischen Zwecken rein auf Suchmaschinen verlassen?**

   a) **Studenten können leicht ihre Neugier verlieren.**

   b) **Studenten werden weniger intelligent, weil sie die Antworten auf ihre Fragen zu leicht finden.**

   c) **Studenten finden nicht mehr originelle, individuelle und persönliche Antworten, die in Büchern und anderen Informationsquellen gefunden werden können.**

Which of these consequences is not mentioned when students rely solely on search engines for academic purposes?

   a) Students can easily lose their sense of curiosity.

   b) Students become less intelligent because they find the answers to their questions too easily.

   c) Students no longer find original, individual and personalized answers that can be found in books and other sources of information.

2) **Welche Informationen sind nun dank des Internets leicht zu finden, die früheren Generationen nicht zur Verfügung standen?**

   a) **Persönliche Informationen wie Geburtsdatum, Bankdaten und Sozialversicherungsnummer**

   b) **Telefonnummer**

   c) **Wohnadresse**

What information is now easy to find due to the internet that was not available in previous generations?

   a) Personal information such as date of birth, bank details and social security number

   b) Phone number

   c) Residence addresse

3) Was ist der Haupt-Negativaspekt von sozialen Netzwerken?

   a) Sie ermutigen Menschen, offen über ihr Privatleben zu sein und Informationen zu teilen, die nützlich für diejenigen sind, die sie für kriminelle und böswillige Zwecke benutzen möchten.

   b) Sie nehmen die Zeit jüngerer Generationen in Anspruch, und diese werden weniger produktiv.

   c) Sie vergleichen unsere Leben mit denen von anderen und erhöhen das Depressionslevel bei jungen Leuten.

What is the main negative aspect of social networking?

   a) It encourages people to be open about their private lives and to share information that is useful to others who wish to use it for criminal or malicious purposes.

   b) It consumes the time of the younger generations and they are becoming less productive.

   c) It compares our lives with those of others and increase the level of depression in young people.

ANSWERS:

   1) B

   2) A

   3) A

GESCHICHTE 11: KANALTUNNEL
STORY 11: CHANNEL TUNNEL

Falls Sie jemals mit dem Auto zwischen Großbritannien und Europa reisen wollen, dann ist das Reisen durch den Kanaltunnel eine einfache Möglichkeit dafür.

If you want to travel by car between Britain and Europe, travelling through the Channel Tunnel is the easy way to do it.

Die Fahrt dorthin auf der Autobahn ist sehr einfach und sie ist gut beschildert.

Getting there on the motorway is very straightforward and it is well-signposted.

Sobald Sie ankommen ist es ein einfacher Prozess und normallerweise geht es glatt.

Once you arrive, it is a simple process and it usually goes smoothly.

Falls Sie vorgebucht haben, können Sie eine automatische Mautstelle benutzen. Sie geben einfach Ihre Buchungs-Referenznummer ein. Sie werden sehen, ob Ihr Zug zur korrekten Zeit fährt und falls nicht, zu welcher Zeit Sie abreisen können. Mit Vorbuchung erlaubt der Eurotunnel alles, was er kann, um sicher zu stellen, dass Sie in dem Zug reisen, den Sie gebucht haben. Es wird Ihnen empfohlen, 45 Minuten vor Ihrer vorgebuchten Abreisezeit anzukommen, obwohl während der Sommermonaten viel Zeit bleibt.

If you have pre-booked, you can use an automatic toll booth. You simply enter your booking reference number. You will see if your train is running on time and, if not, what time you can depart. With pre-booking, Eurotunnel does all that it can to ensure you travel on the train you have booked. You are advised to arrive 45 minutes ahead of your pre-booked departure time, although allow plenty of time during the busy summer months.

Falls Sie nicht vorgebucht haben, können Sie bezahlen, wenn Sie ankommen. Mit dieser Option reisen Sie im nächsten Zug, der Platz hat.

If you have not pre-booked, you can pay when you arrive. With this option, you travel on the next train that has a space.

In beiden Fällen erhalten Sie einen Buchstabencode, zum Aufhängen in Ihrem Auto. Merken Sie sich Ihren Code!

Either way, you will be given a letter code to hang in your car. Remember your code!

Nach der Mautstelle fahren Sie durch zum Terminal. Es ist immer nützlich, die Toilette und die Geschäfte, für einige Last-Minute-Gegenstände, die Sie vergessen haben, zu besuchen. Es gibt eine Palette an Shops, die Parfum, elektronische Geräte, Alkohol und Süßigkeiten anbieten, sowie eine Anzahl an Plätzen zum Essen.

After the toll booth, you go through to the terminal. It's always useful to visit the toilet and to check the shops for any last-minute items you have forgotten. There is a range of shops offering perfume, electrical items, alcohol and sweets, as well as a number of places to eat.

Schauen Sie auf den Bildschirm um herauszufinden, welcher Zug gerade auflädt und welcher Buchstabencode zu diesem Zug gehört. Diese lassen Sie ebenso wissen, wann Ihr Buchstabencode wahrscheinlich aufgerufen wird. Das hilft Ihnen dabei zu wissen, ob Sie Zeit für einen Kaffee oder etwas mehr haben.

Look at the screens to find out which train is loading currently and which letter code relates to that train. They also let you know when your letter is likely to be called. This helps you to know if you have time for a coffee or something more.

Wenn Ihr Buchstabe aufgerufen wird, kehren Sie zu ihrem Auto zurück und folgen Sie den Zeichen. Sie werden durch die Reisepasskontrolle fahren und dann durch einen Sicherheitsbereich, bevor Sie der Warteschlange beitreten, um auf den Zug zu fahren.

When your letter is called, return to your car and follow the signs. You will go through passport control and then through a security area, before joining the queue to drive on to the train.

Diese Warteschlangen sind streng bewacht und Sie müssen sich benehmen und in der Schlange warten.

These queues are closely managed and you must behave yourself and wait in line.

Wenn Sie aufgerufen werden, um in den Zug zu fahren, fahren Sie vorsichtig und befahren Sie den Zug langsam, da er sehr schmal und innen eng ist.

When you are called to board the train, drive carefully and enter the train slowly as it is quite small and narrow inside. Proceed until a member of staff tells you to park.

Beim Parken müssen Sie sorgfältig den Sicherheitsinformationen, die Sie hören, lauschen. Es ist sehr wichtig, dass Sie den Anweisungen folgen – für Ihre eigene Sicherheit und die, der anderen Reisenden. Zum Beispiel sind keine Fotos mit Blitz erlaubt.

When you park, you must listen carefully to the security information you hear. It is very important that you follow the instructions – for your own safety and that of the other travellers. For example, flash photography is not allowed.

Sie werden angewiesen bei Ihrem Auto zu warten, während des Überquerens und Sie müssen ein Autofenster offen lassen.

You are advised to wait by your car during the crossing, and must leave a car window open.

Es gibt Sicherheitsüberprüfungen am Fahrzeug und dann werden Sie die Motoren hören, wie sie für die Reise bereit sind. Die Reise selbst dauert bloß 35 Minuten und die Zeit verfliegt.

There are security checks on the vehicle and then you will hear the engines getting ready to start the journey. The journey itself lasts only 35 minutes, and the time flies by.

Manche Fahrer nutzen diese Zeit zum Schlafen, bevor sie ihre bevorstehende Reise fortführen. Andere nutzen die Zeit, um einen Snack zu essen oder Spiele zu spielen.

Some drivers use this time to sleep before continuing their onward journey. Others use the time to eat a snack or to play games.

Wenn Sie die andere Seite erreichen gibt es weitere Sicherheitsüberprüfungen, bevor sie die Tore öffnen und Sie davon fahren.

When you reach the other side, there are more security checks before they open the doors and you drive away.

Durch den Kanaltunnel zu reisen ist so einfach.

Travelling through the Channel Tunnel is so easy.

Difficult Words

1- Hinkommen – Getting there

2- Gut ausgeschildert – Well-signposted

3- Reibungslos – smoothly

4- Prozess – Process

5- Normalerweise – Usually

6- Mauthäuschen – Toll booth

7- Buchung – Booking

8- Geraten – Advised

9- Platz – Space

10-Nächste(r) – Next

11- Vergessen haben – Have forgotten

12-Süßigkeiten – Sweets

13-Folgen – Follow

14-Schlange – Queue

15-Gemanagt – Managed

Zusammenfassung der Geschichte:

Der Ärmelkanal-Tunnel ist der schnellste und leichteste Weg, zwischen Europa und Großbritannien zu reisen. Diese Geschichte beschreibt den Prozess, wie man reibungslos durch den Tunnel kommt.

Summary of the Story:

The Channel Tunnel is the quickest and easiest way to travel between Europe and Britain. This story describes the process to get through this tunnel smoothly.

Quiz:

1) Wie lange vorher sollte man ankommen, wenn man vorgebucht hat?

 a) 35 Minuten

 b) 45 Minuten

 c) 1 Stunde

How long in advance should you arrive when you have a pre-booked?

 a) 35 minutes

 b) 45 minutes

 c) 1 hour

2) Was kann man im Terminal finden?

 a) Restaurants

 b) Videospiele

 c) Bars

What can be found in the terminal?

 a) Restaurants

 b) Video games

 c) Bars

3) Während der Passage ist es ratsam:

 a) Die Geschäfte auszukundschaften.

 b) Sich zu entspannen und einen Kaffee zu besorgen.

 c) Neben dem Auto zu warten.

During the crossing, you are advised to:

 a) To wander in the shops.

 b) To relax and get a coffee.

 c) To wait next to your car.

ANSWERS:

 1) A

 2) A

 3) C

Hier ist die Landesprognose für die nächsten 12 Stunden.

Here is the country's forecast for the next 12 hours.

Im Norden des Landes ist es heute kalt und nass. Starker Regen ist vorhergesagt, mit bis zu 10cm Niederschlag zwischen Mittag und 16:00 und es gibt ebenso das Risiko von Schneeregen und Hagel. Die Temperatur ist niedrig für die Jahreszeit und da sie in der Nacht abfällt, gibt es das Risiko von Frost. Seien Sie besonders vorsichtig, wenn Sie fahren und halten Sie nach Eis auf der Straße Ausschau.

In the north of the country today, it is cold and wet. Heavy rain is forecast, with up to 10cm falling between midday and 1600, and there is also a risk of sleet and hail. The temperature is low for the time of year and, as night falls, there is a risk of frost. Take extra care if you are driving, and look out for ice on the roads.

Im Westen des Landes ist es am Morgen schön, aber es gibt trotzdem ein hohes Risiko von Regen, besonders am Nachmittag. Seien Sie auf einige Stürme vorbereitet, falls es regnet, mit starken Winden, Sturmböen, Donner und Blitzen. Nehmen Sie einen Regenschirm mit, aber denken Sie daran, ihn nicht zu benutzen, falls Sie Donner hören oder Blitze sehen und halten Sie ihre Haustiere im Haus! Der Abend ist trocken aber noch windig, mit steigenden Temperaturen, so wie es für diese Jahreszeit üblich ist.

The west of the country is looking fair in the morning, but there is still a high risk of rain, especially in the afternoon. Be prepared for some storms if it rains, with strong winds, some gale force, and thunder and lightning. Take an umbrella but remember not to use it if you hear thunder or see lightning, and keep your pets indoors! The evening is dry but still windy, with temperatures rising so that they are normal for the time of year.

Im Osten des Landes wird erwartet, dass es nebelig oder trüb ist, besonders am Morgen. Es fühlt sich feucht, und daher kalt an, aber nicht auf Grund von Regen. Nehmen Sie sich vor starkem Wind und Sturmböen, aus dem Westen kommend, in Acht. Die Temperaturen sind für diese Jahreszeit normal, und die Stürme aus dem Westen werden sich auflösen, bevor sie den Osten erreichen.

The east of the country is expected to be foggy or misty, especially in the morning. It feels damp, and therefore cool, but it is not due to rain at all. Beware of strong winds, some gale force, coming from the west. The temperatures are normal for the time of year and the storms in the west will die out before reaching the east.

Der Süden des Landes genießt schönes Wetter. Es gibt eine leichte Brise und warme Temperaturen, mit keinem Risiko von Regen. Regenfall im Süden bleibt weiterhin niedrig für die Jahreszeit, mit hohen Temperaturen für diese Zeit. Auf Grund der hohen Temperaturen, stellen Sie sicher, Wasser mit sich zu nehmen, wenn Sie raus gehen. Beachten Sie, dass Ihre Haustiere und Kinder keinem Risiko eines Sonnenbrandes oder einer Dehydration ausgesetzt sind.

The south of the country is enjoying fine weather. There is a light breeze and warm temperatures, with no risk of rain. Rainfall in the south continues to be low for the time of year, with the temperatures high for the time of year. Because of the high temperatures, make sure you take water with you when you go out. Make sure your pets and children are not at risk of getting sunburn or dehydrated.

Die Wetterprognose für morgen sieht schön und trocken aus.

The forecast for tomorrow looks fine and dry.

Difficult Words

1- Vorhersage – Forecast

2- Nass – Wet

3- Regen – Rain

4- Graupel – Sleet

5- Hagel – Hail

6- Nacht – Night

7- Frost – Frost

8- Vorsicht – Care

9- Sonnenbrand – Sunburn

10-Stürme – Storms

11- Donner – Thunder

12-Blitz – Lightning

13-Windig – Windy

14-Trocken – Dry

15-Neblig – Foggy

Zusammenfassung der Geschichte:

Diese Geschichte beschreibt das Wetter im Norden, Süden, Osten und Westen eines Landes mit Empfehlungen für die Bewohner des Landes.

Summary of the Story:

This story describes the weather in the north, south, east and west of a country with recommendations for the people of that country.

Quiz:

1) Warum sollten Autofahrer im Norden des Landes achtsam sein?

    a) Weil das Risiko von Frost auf der Straße besteht.

    b) Weil starke Regenfälle vorausgesagt sind

    c) Weil auf den Straßen viel Nebel herrschen wird

Why drivers should be careful in the north part of the country?

    a) Because there is risk of frost on the road.

    b) Because a heavy rain is forecasted.

    c) Because there will be a lot of fog on the roads.

2) Was sind die Ratschläge für Leute, die im Süden des Landes leben?

    a) Einen Schirm mitnehmen, aber nicht benutzen, wenn es donnert und blitzt.

    b) Sonnenbrand meiden und Wasser trinken.

    c) Die Tiere drinnen behalten, da starke Winde auftreten.

What is the advice for the people living in the south of the country?

    a) Bring your umbrella, but don't use it if there is thunder or lightning.

    b) Avoid sun burn and stay hydrated.

    c) Keep the animals inside, because wind will be strong.

3) Welche Temperaturen liegen im Osten des Landes vor?

    a) Die Temperaturen sind hoch für diese Jahreszeit.

    b) Die Temperaturen sind für diese Jahreszeit niedrig.

    c) Die Temperaturen sind für diese Jahreszeit normal.

What is the temperature in the east of the country?

    a) The temperature is high for the time of year.

    b) The temperature is low for the time of year.

    c) The temperatures are normal for the time of year.

ANSWERS:

    1) A

    2) B

    3) C

GESCHICHTE 13: EIN BESCHÄFTIGER TAG IN DEN FERIEN (2)
STORY 13: A BUSY DAY IN THE HOLIDAYS (2)

Henry und ich sprechen darüber, wie arbeiten – und Arbeiten erledigen – dir dabei hilft, Belohnungen oder, vielleicht, Geld zu erhalten.

Henry and I talk about how working - and doing jobs - helps you to earn treats or, perhaps, money. He remembers cleaning the car and being taken swimming as his reward.

Er wacht auf – voll mit Energie und dem Willen beschäftigt zu sein, wie immer – und er fragt, welche Arbeiten er heute machen kann.

He gets up – full of energy and wanting to be busy, as always – and asks what jobs he can do today.

Nach dem Frühstück starten wir damit darüber nachzudenken, was er tatsächlich tun kann, angesichts seiner Größe. Dann reden wir darüber, was heute gemacht werden muss.

After breakfast, we start by thinking about what he can actually do, given his size. Then we talk about what needs to be done today.

Ich sage, wir brauchen Milch und Brot vom Lebensmittelgeschäft im Dorf. Henry sagt, der Rasen muss gemäht werden und wir müssen mit dem Hund spazieren gehen. Ich erwähne, dass das Badezimmer gut gereinigt und das Haus staubgesaugt werden muss,

I say we need some milk and bread from the grocery store in the village. Henry says the lawn needs mowing and we must walk the dog. I mention that the bathroom needs a good clean and the house needs to be hoovered.

Wir vereinbaren, dass Henry den Hund zum Lebensmittelgeschäft Gassi führen kann, ihn draußen anbindet, dann rein geht und die Milch und das Brot kauft. Er geht mit einem aufgeregten Hund und einem Sprung in seinen Schritten los. Ich finde die Gummihandschuhe und die Reinigungsprodukte und beginne das Badezimmer zu reinigen. Das ist die Arbeit, die ich am wenigsten mag, aber ich kann nicht Henry fragen, das zu tun. Als ich fertig bin, nehme ich den Staubsauger aus dem Schrank und sauge durch das Haus. Überall sieht und fühlt es sich viel sauberer an, als ich fertig bin.

We agree that Henry can walk the dog to the grocery store, tie him up outside, then go in and buy the milk and the bread. He sets off with an excited dog and a spring in his step. I find the rubber gloves and cleaning products, and set to cleaning the bathroom. This is the job I like the least, but I can't ask Henry to do it. When I finish, I then take the hoover from the cupboard and hoover around the house. Everywhere looks and feels much cleaner when I finish.

Henry kommt mit der Milch, dem Brot und dem Hund nach Hause und einer Tafel Schokolade, für uns beide später. Großartige Idee!

Henry comes home with the milk and the bread, and the dog, and a bar of chocolate for each of us to have later. Great idea!

Wir beschließen, den Rasen gemeinsam zu mähen. Es braucht seine Zeit. Ich schiebe den Mäher und Henry hakt das geschnittene Grass zusammen. Er bringt es auf einem Stapel in der Ecke, außerhalb des Weges.

We decide to mow the lawn together. It takes a while. I push the mower and Henry rakes up the grass cuttings. He puts them in a pile in the corner, out of the way.

Es ist fast Mittagszeit und wir haben beinahe unsere Arbeiten beendet. Henry richtet den Tisch und ich mache uns Sandwiches. Wir setzten uns hin und essen zusammen Mittag.

It's almost lunch time and we have almost finished our jobs. Henry sets the table and I make us a sandwich. We sit down to eat lunch together.

Wir versuchen zu beschließen, was wir am Nachmittag machen und ich stimme zu, dass wir beide zu müde sind und nur zu Hause bleiben wollen und entspannen und unsere Arbeit bewundern. Und natürlich unsere Schokolade zu essen.

We try to decide what to do in the afternoon and agree that we are both too tired and just want to stay at home and relax, and admire our work. And eat our chocolate, of course.

Eine weitere großartige Idee!

Another great idea!

Difficult Words

1- Beschäftigt – Busy

2- Immer – Always

3- Tatsächlich – Actually

4- Brot – Bread

5- Rasen – Lawn

6- Mähen – Mowing

7- Anbinden – To tie

8- Gummihandschuhe – Robber gloves

9- Schrank – Cupboard

10-Sauberer – Cleaner

11- Großartige Idee – Great idea

12-Zusammen – Together

13-Gras – Grass

14-Ecke – Corner

15-Müde – Tired

Zusammenfassung der Geschichte:

Henry, ein energiegeladener 8-jähriger Junge, mag nun das Prinzip von Arbeiten für eine Belohnung. Sein Vater und er nutzen die Gelegenheit, zusammen zu entscheiden, welche Aufgaben am Tag ausgeführt werden sollen.

Summary of the Story:

Henry, an energetic 8-year-old boy, now loves the concept of working in return for reward. He and his father take the opportunity to decide together on the tasks to be carried out for the day.

Quiz:

1) Was macht Henrys Vater, während Henry zum Lebensmittelgeschäft geht?

a) Er mäht den Rasen.

b) Er macht das Badezimmer sauber.

c) Er entspannt und isst Schokolade.

What does Henry's father do while Henry's going to the grocery store?

a) He mows the lawn.

b) He cleans the bathroom.

c) He relaxes and eats chocolate.

2) Wer staubsaugt?

a) Henry

b) Henrys Vater

c) Niemand staubsaugt.

Who is vacuuming?

a) Henry

b) Henry's father

c) No one is doing the vacuum.

3) Zu welcher Tageszeit beenden Henry und sein Vater die Arbeit?

a) Am Morgen

b) Am Ende des Nachmittags

c) Um die Mittagszeit

What time of the day does Henry and his father finish working?

a) In morning

b) At the end of the afternoon

c) Around lunch time

ANSWERS:

1) B

2) B

3) C

GESCHICHTE 14: SMARTPHONES
STORY 14: SMARTPHONES

Es ist gerade einmal ein Jahrzehnt, seit das Smartphone von Apple erfunden wurde. Handys waren davor bereits verbreitet, aber dann änderten Smartphone, wie wir miteinander kommunizieren.

It is just over a decade since the smartphone was invented by Apple. Mobile phones were common enough before then but the smartphone changes how we communicate with each other.

Die Anzahl an Sprachnachrichten, getätigt auf einem Handy, fielen zum ersten Mal in 2017 – neben der Tatsache, dass wir ständig mit unseren Geräten verbunden sind.

The number of voice calls made on mobile phones fell for the first time in 2017 - despite the fact we are hooked on our devices.

Im Gesamten besitzen 78% aller Erwachsenen nun ein Smartphone.

A total of 78% of all adults now owns a smartphone.

Im Durchschnitt wird geglaubt, dass Menschen alle 12 Minuten auf ihr Handy schauen, wenn sie wach sind.

On average, it is believed that people check their phone once every 12 minutes when they're awake.

Zwei von fünf Erwachsenen schauen auf ihr Handy innerhalb von 5 Minuten, nachdem sie aufwachen und ein dritter überprüft sein Handy direkt vor dem Einschlafen.

Two in five adults look at their phone within five minutes of waking up, and a third check their phones just before falling asleep.

Es versteht sich, dass ein hoher Prozentsatz (71%) der Menschen ihr Handy nie abschalten und 78% der Menschen sagen, sie können nicht ohne leben.

It is understood that a high percentage (71%) of people never turn off their phone and 78% openly say they cannot live without it.

Dreiviertel der Menschen betrachten Sprachnachrichten noch immer als eine wichtige Funktion von ihren Handys, mehr (92%) glauben, dass Web Browsen entscheidend ist und sie verwenden ihre Handys, um dies zu tun.

Three-quarters of people still regard voice calling as an important function of their phones, more (92%) believe web browsing is crucial, and they choose to use their phone to do this.

Es wird geglaubt, dass die totale Anzahl an Anrufen, getätigt auf Handys, in 2017 um 1,7% fällt , obwohl sie zu tätigen so günstig ist, wie es nie zuvor war.

It is believed that the total number of calls made on mobiles fell by 1.7% in 2017, even though making them is the cheapest it has ever been.

Das bedeutet nicht notwendigerweise, dass Menschen weniger miteinander reden, aber dass sie auf unterschiedlichen Wegen kommunizieren.

That does not necessarily mean people are talking to each other less, but they are talking in different ways.

Es herrscht Einigkeit darüber, dass das Leben der Menschen sich über das letzte Jahrzehnt, verändert hat, durch den Aufschwung des Smartphone, zusammen mit besserem Anschluss an das Internet und neuen Dienstleistungen. Wir können unterwegs mehr tun, als jemals zuvor.

It is agreed that, over the last decade, people's lives have been transformed by the rise of the smartphone, together with better access to the internet and new services. We can do more on the move than ever before.

Menschen sind sich einig, ihr Smartphone sei ihr konstanter Begleiter, aber manche finden sich selbst überlastet, wenn sie online sind, oder frustriert, wenn sie es nicht sind.

People agree their smartphone is their constant companion, but some are finding themselves overloaded when online, or frustrated when they're not.

Innerhalb von Familien hängen verschiedene Mitglieder vorm Smartphone aus verschiedenen Gründen ab. Der eine wird es zum Überprüfen von sozialen Netzwerden und dem Wetter nutzen und um Einkaufslisten zu speichern; ein anderer wird es zum Buchen von Taxis und zum E-Mails lesen verwenden. Andere benutzen es, um Spiele zu spielen, im Internet zu suchen und YouTube zu sehen.

Within families, different members depend on their smartphones for different reasons. One may use it for checking social media and the weather, and to store shopping lists; another will use it to book taxis and read emails. Others use it to play games, search the internet, and watch YouTube.

Und manche Familien haben Regeln dafür, wann es höflich ist, ein Smartphone zu benutzen und wann es außerhalb der Sichtweite gehalten werden soll.

And some families have rules for when it is polite to use a smartphone and when it should be kept out of sight.

Haben Sie irgendwelche Regeln gesetzt, wann und wo Sie Ihr Handy benutzen?

Have you set any rules for when and where you use your phone?

Difficult Words

1- Jahrzehnt – Decade

2- Sprachanrufe – Voice Calls

3- Durchschnittlich – Average

4- Wach – Awake

5- Aufwachen – Waking up

6- Einschlafen – Falling asleep

7- Hoch – High

8- Öffentlich – Openly

9- Leben – To live

10- Browsing – Browsing

11- Essentiell – Crucial

12- Fiel – Fell

13- Überlastung – Overload

14- Wetter – Weather

15- Einkaufslisten – Shopping lists

Zusammenfassung der Geschichte:

Es ist über ein Jahrzehnt her, dass das Smartphone von Apple erfunden worden ist. Auch wenn Handys vor dieser Erfindung existiert haben, ändern Smartphones die Art und Weise, wie wir miteinander kommunizieren. Diese Geschichte beschreibt die Ergebnisse einer Studie bezüglich des Gebrauchs von Smartphones heute.

Summary of the Story:

It has now been over a decade since the smartphone was invented by Apple. Even if cellphones existed before this invention, smartphones are changing the way we communicate with each other. This story describes the results of a study on the use of smartphones today.

Quiz:

1) Wie oft prüfen Menschen im Durchschnitt ihr Handy?

a) Um die 5 Minuten

b) Jede 12 Minuten

c) Jede 15 Minuten

On average, how often do people check their phone?

a) Around every 5 minutes

b) Around every 12 minutes

c) Around every 15 minutes

2) Wie viel Prozent aller Erwachsenen überprüft ihr Handy in der Minute, in der sie aufwachen?

a) Zwei von fünf Erwachsenen

b) Drei von fünf Erwachsenen

c) Ein von fünf Erwachsenen

What is the percentage of adults who checks their phone the moment they wake up?

a) Two in five adults

b) Three in five adults

c) One in five adults

3) Welche der folgenden Aussagen ist wahr?

a) Nur ein Viertel der Leute betrachtet Sprachanrufe immernoch als eine wichtige Funktion ihres Handys.

b) Mehr als Dreiviertel der Menschen hält Webbrowsing für essentiell.

c) Sprachanrufe werden bei Handys für wichtiger gehalten als Surfen im Internet.

Which of these statements is true?

a) Only a quarter of people still consider voice calls an important function of their phones.

b) More than three-quarters of people consider web browsing to be crucial.

c) On phones, voice calling is considered more important than browsing the web.

ANSWERS:

1) B

2) A

3) B

Chester ist die Bezirksstadt von Cheshire, welches im Nordwesten von England, sehr nahe zur walisischen Grenze liegt.

Chester is the county town of Cheshire, which is in the north-west of England, very close to the Welsh border. Some British people are uncertain whether Chester is in England or Wales, but it is definitely in England.

Als Kreisstadt ist sie seit fast 2000 Jahren eine Stadt.

As well as being the county town, it has been a city for nearly 2,000 years.

Chester ist eine römische Stadt und Sie können heutzutage noch immer viele römische Plätze sehen. Der wichtigste der Plätze ist die Stadtmauer, welche zu den am meisten intakten Stadtmauern in Großbritannien zählt. Sie können einfach um die Mauern herum gehen; diese waren die Mauern des ursprünglichen Forts. Sie sind um die 3km lang und umrundeten die ursprüngliche Stadt. Sie wurden zwischen 70 n.Chr. und 80 n.Chr. erbaut. Sie können ebenso die Überreste eines römischen Amphitheaters sehen. Besuchen Sie auf jeden Fall das römische Geschichts-Museum, während Sie dort sind.

Chester is a Roman town and you can still see many Roman sites there today. The most important of the sites is the City Walls which are the most intact city walls in Britain. You can easily walk around the walls; these were the walls of the original fort. They are about 3km long and surround the original town. They were built between 70 AD and 80 AD. You can also see the remains of a Roman amphitheatre. Make sure you visit the Roman History Museum while you're there.

Der Fluss Dee läuft durch Chester und es ist ein Zentrum zum Segeln, Kanu fahren und für Boot-Ausflüge. Es ist auch eine liebliche Umgebung für lange Spaziergänge und Picknicks. Die Römer nannten Chester Deva, nach dem Fluss Dee. Der Fluss war eine signifikante Handelsroute für die Römer und Deva hatte einen langen Hafen, um die Güter zu bringen, die die Stadt benötigte. Der Hafen ist nicht mehr vorhanden.

The River Dee runs through Chester and it is a centre for sailing, canoeing, and boat trips. It is also a lovely setting for long walks and picnics. The Romans called Chester Deva after the River Dee. The river was a significant trade route for the Romans and Deva had a large harbour to bring in the goods the city needed. The harbour is no longer there.

Die Konstruktion von Chester Castle begann im 11. Jahrhundert n. Chr., zur gleichen Zeit wie bei der Kathedrale. Die Kathedrale wurde schließlich im Jahr 1535 n. Chr. beendet.

The construction of Chester Castle started in the 11th century AD, at the same time as the cathedral. The cathedral was finally finished in 1535 AD.

Chester ist vielleicht am berühmtesten für seine schwarzen und weißen Gebäude, die übereinander stehen. Sie werden „The Rows" genannt. Heute beinhalten diese das Haupt-Shoppingcenter und ein Grand-Hotel, The Grosvenor.

Chester is perhaps most famous for its black and white buildings which sit on top of each other. They are called 'The Rows'. Today, these contain the main shopping centre and a grand hotel, The Grosvenor.

Das Zentrum der Stadt ist mit einem Kreuz markiert, welches auf jenem Punkt steht, wo sich die 4 römischen Hauptstraßen trafen.

The centre of the city is marked with a Cross, which stands at the point where the 4 main Roman roads meet.

Falls Sie irgendwo etwas anderes besuchen wollen, mit viel Geschichte, zum entdecken, denken Sie an Chestern.

If you want to visit somewhere a little different with a huge amount of history to explore, think of Chester.

Es ist hübsch.

It's beautiful.

Difficult Words

1- Grenze – Border

2- Kreisstadt – County town

3- Stadt – Town

4- Mauern – Walls

5- über – About

6- Gebaut – Built

7- Überreste – Remains

8- Kreuz – Cross

9- Segeln – Sailing

10-Bootsausflüge – Boat trips

11- Hafen – Harbour

12-Festung – Castle

13-Beendet – Finished

14-Bauten – Buildings

15-Die Reihen – The Rows

Zusammenfassung der Geschichte:

Chester ist eine Kreisstadt in England, die im Nordwesten des Landes liegt. Diese Geschichte beschreibt die römische Vergangenheit dieser Stadt und zieht Verbindungen zu derzeitigen Standorten.

Summary of the Story:

Chester is the county town of England located in the north-west of the country. This story describes the Roman history of this city and makes connections to its current locations.

Quiz:

1) Wie viele Kilometer lang ist die Stadtmauer?

    a) 10 km

    b) 5 km

    c) 3 km

How many kilometers long is The City Wall?

    a) 10 km

    b) 5 km

    c) 3 km

2) In der Nähe des Flusses Dee können wir derzeit finden:

    a) Einen großen Hafen, der Güter einbringt.

    b) Ein Center für Segeln, Kanufahren und Bootsausflüge.

    c) Eine große Kathedrale.

Near the Dee River, we can currently find:

    a) A large port to bring in the goods.

    b) A center for sailing, canoeing, and boat trips.

    c) A big cathedral.

3) Welche dieser Aussagen ist falsch?

    a) Der Bau der Festung von Chester hat zur selben Zeit wie der Bau der Kathedrale begonnen.

    b) Chester ist bekannt für seine bunten Gebäude.

    c) Die Kathedrale wurde 1535 n. Chr. fertiggestellt.

Which of these statements is false?

    a) The construction of Chester Castle started at the same time as the cathedral.

    b) Chester is famous for its colorful buildings.

    c) The cathedral was finished in 1535 AD.

ANSWERS:

    1) C

    2) B

    3) B

Sarah und Peter sitzen mit einem Glass Wein jeden Abend zusammen. Henry schläft im Bett und Charlie, der Hund, schläft am Boden zu deren Füßen.

Sarah and Peter sit down with a glass of wine one evening. Henry is asleep in bed and Charlie, the dog, is asleep on the floor at their feet.

„Willst du dieses Jahr im Urlaub weg", fragt Peter Sarah. „Und wenn du willst, wohin willst du gehen?"

"Do you want to go on holiday this year," Peter asks Sarah. "And if you do, where do you want to go?"

Sarah denkt für einige Momente nach und sagt, „Ja, es würde schön sein, weg zu kommen. Meine neue Arbeit ist großartig, aber ich bin bereit für eine Pause."

Sarah thinks for a few moments and says, "Yes, it will be nice to get away. My new job is great but I am ready for a break."

„Wohin sollen wir dann gehen? Irgendwelche Ideen?" fragt Peter nochmals.

"Where shall we go then? Any ideas?" asks Peter again.

Beide machen einige Vorschläge. Griechenland, Italien, Portugal. Vielleicht weiter weg nach Ägypten, Tunesien, Türkei oder sogar Vereinigte Staaten. Oder vielleicht England?

They both make some suggestions. Greece, Italy, Portugal. Perhaps further afield to Egypt, Tunisia, Turkey, or even the United States. Or maybe England?

Dann fragt Sarah, „Können wir zuerst entscheiden, was wir im Urlaub machen wollen, bevor wir entscheiden, wohin wir gehen? Ich meine, wir müssen an Henry denken und was er genießen würde, nicht nur, was wir tun wollen."

Then Sarah asks, "Can we decide what we want to do on holiday before we decide where to go? I mean, we have to think about Henry and what he will enjoy, not just what we want to do."

Peter sagt zustimmend, „Gut, wenn es nach mir ginge, ich könne einfach gehen und irgendwo warm und sonnig an einem Strand liegen, schwimmen gehen, Bier trinken und keine Hausarbeiten tun zu

müssen." Dann fügt er hinzu, „Aber Henry würde das nicht genießen, oder? Er muss beschäftigt und aktiv sein. Ach je, Ich kann an nichts denken, dass wir alle genießen und davon profitieren werden."

Peter agrees saying, "Well, if it were up to me, I could just go and lie on a beach somewhere warm and sunny, go swimming, drink beer, and not have to do any house work." The he adds, "But Henry wouldn't enjoy that, would he? He needs to be busy and active. Oh dear, I can't think of anything that we will all enjoy and benefit from."

Sie sitzen in Stille und bedenken, was sie tun können, dass Henry glücklich machen wird und ebenso deren Leben einfacher.

They each sit in silence and consider what they can do that will make Henry happy, and also make their lives easy.

Vielleicht, ruft Peter heraus, „Disneyland Paris! Was ist mit Disneyland Paris? Wir sagen immer, wir sollten hingehen und ich weiß, Henry würde beschäftig sein und eine fantastische Zeit haben. Was denkst du?"

Eventually, Peter shouts out, "Disneyland Paris! What about Disneyland Paris? We always say we should go and I know Henry would be busy and would have a fantastic time. What do you think?"

Sarah dreht sich lächeln zu Peter und sagt, „Ich denke, das würde perfekt sein. Wir würden alle beschäftig sein und die ganze Zeit Spaß haben. Henry wird seine ganze Energie verwenden und es wird eine großartige Erfahrung zum Erinnern sein. Was für ein großartiger Vorschlag. Lass uns beginnen, zu plannen!"

Sarah turns to Peter smiling and says, "I think that would be perfect. We would all be busy and having fun at the same time. Henry will use up a lot of his energy, and it will be a great experience to remember. What a great suggestion. Let's start planning!"

Difficult Words

1- Wein – Wine

2- Glas – Glass

3- Schläft – Asleep

4- Füße – Feet

5- Fragt – Asks

6- Trinken – Drink

7- Glücklich – Happy

8- Ruft – Shouts

9- Spaß haben – Having fun

10-Planen – Planning

11- Leben – Life

12-Erwägen – Consider

13-Wir werden es genießen – We will enjoy

14-Wenige Momente – Few moments

15-Pause – Break

Zusammenfassung der Geschichte:

Sarah und ihr Ehemann Peter denken über ihren nächsten Urlaub nach. Es gibt viel zu bedenken, wenn man entscheiden möchte, wohin es gehen soll, weil jeder verschiedene Aktivitäten unternehmen möchte. Sie müssen auch bedenken, was ihr Sohn Henry möglicherweise unternehmen möchte. Was werden sie für den diesjährigen Urlaub wählen?

Summary of the Story:

Sarah and her husband Peter are thinking about their next vacation. There is a lot to consider when deciding where to go, as everyone wants to do different activities and they also have to think about what their son Henry would like to do. What will they choose this year for the holidays?

Quiz:

1) Wie möchte Peter gern den Urlaub verbringen?
   a) Er würde gern nach Ägypten reisen.

   b) Er möchte nach Disneyland.

   c) Er möchte am Strand liegen, schwimmen gehen und Bier trinken.

What would Peter like to do for the holidays?
   a) He would like to go in Egypt.

   b) He would like to go at Disneyland.

   c) He would like to lie on a beach, go swimming and drink beer.

2) Warum scheint Disneyland die perfekte Idee zu sein?
   a) Weil alle zur gleichen Zeit beschäftigt sein und Spaß haben würden.

   b) Weil Henry davon träumt, dorthin zu reisen.

   c) Weil sie dann während des Urlaubs nicht auf Henry aufpassen müssen.

Why Disneyland Paris seams a perfect idea?
   a) Because they would all be busy and having fun at the same time.

   b) Because Henry dreams to go there.

   c) Because they won't have to take care of Henry during the Holidays.

3) Welches Land schlagen Sarah und Peter nicht vor?
   a) Portugal

   b) Kanada

   c) Türkei

Which country is not proposed by Sarah and Peter?
   a) Portugal

   b) Canada

   c) Turkey

ANSWERS:
   1) C

   2) A

   3) B

Die Entscheidung ist getroffen. Sie fahren nach Disneyland Paris in den Urlaub. Es ist Zeit mit der Planung zu beginnen.

The decision is made. They're going to Disneyland Paris for their holiday. It's time to start planning.

Sarah und Peter gehen online, um über Disneyland Paris zu recherchieren. Sie beginnen damit, wie man dorthin kommt.

Sarah and Peter go online to start researching Disneyland Paris. They start with how to get there.

Es scheint, als gibt es eine Vielzahl an Optionen. Sie können entweder fliegen und dann den Bus nehmen, mit dem Zug mit einigen Umstiegen reisen oder selbst fahren. Sie mögen die Idee selbst zu fahren, also beschließen sie, dass es dies ist, was sie tun werden. Es gibt genügend Parkplätze, also wird das kein Problem sein.

It seems they have a number of options. They can either fly and then take a bus, travel by train with some changes, or drive there themselves. They like the idea of driving so they decide that is what they will do. There is plenty of parking so that won't be a problem.

Dann beginnen sie nach Unterkünften zu sehen und beschließen, dass es für Henry mehr Spaß sein wird, wenn sie in einem der Disneyland Hotels übernachten. Als sie danach zu sehen beginnen, merken sie, dass sie alle sehr verschieden und riesig sind. In einem der Resort-Hotels zu bleiben, bedeutet, dass sie jeden Tag in den Park gehen können, aber falls notwendig, abends einen Bus zurück nehmen, wenn Henrys Beine nicht mehr gehen wollen.

They then start to look at accommodation and decide it will be more fun for Henry if they stay in one of the Disneyland Hotels. When they start looking at them, they realise that they are all very different, and that they're huge. Staying in one of the resort hotels means that they can walk into the park each day but, if necessary, take a bus back in the evening when Henry's legs won't work anymore.

Sie sehen nach den verschiedenen Hotels und unterschiedlichen Themen. Sie mögen das Aussehen vom Newport Bay Club, denken aber, dass Henry das Hotel Cheyenne bevorzugen wird, da er Cowboys

und Indianer liebt. Also ist es das Hotel Cheyenne. Sie sehen nach dem Datum, den Kosten und der Verfügbarkeit.

They look at the different hotels and their different themes. They like the look of the Newport Bay Club but think that Henry will prefer the Hotel Cheyenne as he loves cowboys and Indians. So, the Hotel Cheyenne it is. They look at dates, costs, and availability.

Dann beginnen sie darüber nachzudenken, wie lange sie bleiben werden. Neben den 2 Plätzen des Parks die es zu besichtigen und genießen gibt, beginnen sie im Detail zu erkunden, was genau es dort zu machen gibt. Fahrten, Shows, Charaktere treffen und die Atmosphäre Aufsaugen. Sie beschließen 3 Nächte mit 4 Tagen im Park werden genau richtig sein.

They then start to think about how long they will go for. With the 2 sides of the park to visit and enjoy, they start to look in detail at what exactly there is to do. Rides, shows, characters to meet, and the atmosphere to soak up. They decide 3 nights with 4 days in the park will be just right.

Sie sind gerade dabei, die Buchung zu machen, als sie stoppen und merken, dass sie auch an Charlie denken müssen. Was werden sie mit Charlie tun, während sie fort sind? Sie kennen niemanden, der Hunde gerne genug hat, um nach ihm zu sehen und sie kennen keine nahen Tierpensionen.

They are about to make a booking when they stop and realise that they have Charlie to think about. What will they do with Charlie while they are away? They don't know anybody who likes dogs enough to look after him for them, and they don't know any kennels nearby.

Dann bemerken sie, dass Disneyland Paris ein Haustier-Zentrum für Besucher des Parks hat. Perfekte Lösung – Charlie wird auch einen Urlaub haben!

Then they notice that Disneyland Paris has a pet centre for the pets of people visiting the park. Perfect solution – Charlie will have a holiday too!

Difficult Words

1- Beginnen – To start

2- Riesig – Huge

3- Laufen – To walk

4- Der Abend – The evening

5- Beine – Legs

6- Verfügbarkeit – Availability

7- Seiten – Sides

8- Fahrgeschäfte – Rides

9- Shows – Shows

10-Charaktere – Characters

11- Atmosphäre – Atmosphere

12-Aufsaugen – To soak up

13-Tierpensionen – Kennels

14-Nahebei – Nearby

15-Haustiere – Pets

Zusammenfassung der Geschichte:

Die Entscheidung ist getroffen. Sarah und Peters Familie wird den Urlaub in Disneyland Paris verbringen. Nun müssen sie ihren Besuch planen.

Summary of the Story:

The decision is made. Sarah and Peter's family will go to Disneyland Paris for their vacation. Now they have to plan their visit.

Quiz:

1) Was ist der Hauptvorteil, wenn sie in einem der Resorthotels des Parks übernachten?

    a) Sie können jeden Tag zu Fuß in den Park gehen und zurück den Bus nehmen.

    b) Sie sparen Zeit, da sie sich schon direkt vor Ort befinden.

    c) Sie werden Geld sparen, denn die Hotels im Park sind günstiger als außerhalb des Parks.

What is the main advantage of staying in one of the resort hotel of the park?

    a) They can walk into the park each day and come back at their hotel by bus.

    b) They will save time because they are already on the site.

    c) They will save money because hotels of the site are cheaper than outside of the park.

2) Wie lang ist ihr Aufenthalt?

    a) 4 Nächte und 3 Tage

    b) 2 Nächte und 3 Tage

    c) 3 Nächte und 4 Tage

How long is their stay?

    a) 4 nights and 3 days

    b) 2 nights and 3 days

    c) 3 nights and 4 days

3) Wer ist Charlie?

    a) Ein Freund von Henry

    b) Der Familienhund

    c) Die Katze der Familie

Who is Charlie?

    a) The friend of Henry

    b) The family's dog

    c) The family's cat

ANSWERS:

    1) A

    2) C

    3) B

Sie machen sich auf den Weg und nach mehreren Stunden des Reisens spulen sie die Route automatisch ab und machen sich auf denWeg zu dem Hotel in Disneyland Paris. Henry ist so aufgeregt! Charlie ist sich nicht bewusst, dass er auch einen Urlaub hat, aber er ist sowieso aufgeregt.

They set off and after several hours of travelling, they pull off the autoroute and make their way to their hotel at Disneyland Paris. Henry is so excited! Charlie is not aware that he is having a holiday too, but he is excited anyway.

Sarah, Peter und Henry buchen im Hotel Cheyenne ein und lassen Charlie für eine Weile im Auto. Das Zimmer ist erstaunlich und Henry ist sehr aufgeregt, in einem Etagenbett zu schlafen. Er kann sich nicht entscheiden, ob er in der oberen oder unteren Etage schläft. Was für eine Entscheidung!

Sarah, Peter and Henry book in to the Hotel Cheyenne and leave Charlie in the car for a while. The room is amazing and Henry is very excited to be sleeping in a bunk bed. He can't decide whether to sleep on the top or the bottom bunk. What a decision!

Nach ein paar Minuten beschließen sie, zurück zum Auto zu gehen und Charlie einzusammeln.

After a few minutes, they decide to go back to the car and collect Charlie.

„Sollen wir jetzt zum Park gehen und Charlie später in sein Hotel einbuchen?" schlägt Peter an Henry vor. Sie gehen zum Park und finden das Tierzentrum, welches beim Besucherparkplatz liegt. Sie buchen Charlie ein und brechen zum Park auf, wissend, dass er in seinem Hotel auch glücklich sein wird.

"Shall we head to the park now and check Charlie in to his hotel?" Peter suggests to Henry. They go to the park and find the animal centre which is in the visitor parking area. They check Charlie in and head off towards the park, knowing that he will be happy in his hotel too.

Sie können überall um sie herum die fröhliche Disney-Musik hören und gehen mit einem Sprung im deren Schritten. Sie kommen am Haupteingang an und gehen durch die Taschenkontrollen.

They can hear the happy Disney music all around them and walk with a spring in their step. They arrive at the main entrance and go through the bag security checks.

Dann müssen sie eine Entscheidung treffen: Entweder in den Hauptpark gehen – der ursprüngliche Disney-Park – und die traditionellen Disney-Fahrten machen, oder zu den Walt Disney Studios gehen. Was für eine Wahl!

Then they have to make a decision: whether to go into the main park - the original Disney Park - and do the traditional Disney rides, or whether to go in to Walt Disney Studios. What a choice!

Also fragt Sarah Henry, „Wo sollen wir beginnen, Henry?"

So, Sarah asks Henry, "Where shall we start, Henry?"

Für Henry ist es eine einfache Entscheidung. „Lass uns in den Disney Park gehen und nach einigen Charakteren suchen."

For Henry, it's an easy decision. "Let's go into the Disney Park and look for some characters."

Also gehen sie dorthin.

So that's where they go.

Sofort sehen sie Pluto nahe der Eisenbahnstation am Anfang der Hauptstraße und er ist von lächelnden Menschen umgeben. Sie beschließen an ihm vorbei zu gehen und sehen plötzlich, gegenüber von ihnen Mickey und Minnie Mouse gehen. Dieses Mal gibt es keine Menschenmenge und Henry rennt rüber, um ihnen hallo zu sagen.

Straightaway, they see Pluto near the railway station at the start of Main Street, and he is surrounded by smiling people. They decide to carry on past him and suddenly see, walking towards them, Mickey and Minnie Mouse. This time, there is no crowd of people and Henry runs towards them to say hello.

Mickey und Minnie lächeln und winken und geben Henry ein High Five. Und Peter macht ein Foto von den dreien zusammen. Henry erzählt ihnen allen über Charlie und das Hotel, in dem sie bleiben und Mickey und Minnie hören lächelnd mit Interesse zu.

Mickey and Minnie smile and wave and 'high five' Henry. And Peter takes a photograph of the three of them together. Henry tells them all about Charlie and the hotel they're stating at and Mickey and Minnie listen with interest, smiling.

Henry ist so aufgeregt und hört nicht auf, zu reden.

Henry is so excited and doesn't stop talking.

Difficult Words

1- Sie brechen auf – They set off

2- Erstaunlich – Amazing

3- Etagenbett – Bunk bed

4- Sammeln/einsammeln – To collect

5- Sie checken ein – They check in

6- Sich aufmachen – Head off

7- Hören – To hear

8- Haupteingang – Main entrance

9- Taschen – Bags

10-Lächelnd – Smiling

11- Rennt – Runs

12-Interesse – Interest

13-Umgeben – Surrounded

14-Wissend – Knowing

15-Zimmer – Room

Zusammenfassung der Geschichte:

Der Stichtag für Sarah, Peter und Henry ist gekommen, und endlich erreichen sie Disneyland Paris, wo sie ihren Urlaub verbringen. Henry ist so aufgeregt über dieses Abenteuer.

Summary of the Story:

It's finally D-Day for Sarah, Peter and Henry since they finally arrived at Disneyland Paris for the holidays. Henry is so excited by this new adventure.

Quiz:

1) **Wie fühlen sich Peter und Henry, wenn sie Charlie im Tierzentrum abgeben?**

   a) **Glücklich, weil sie wissen, dass Charlie in diesem Hotel auch glücklich sein wird.**

   b) **Ängstlich, weil Charlie noch nie in einem Hotel ohne sie war.**

   c) **Aufgeregt, weil es Charlies erste Erfahrung in einem Hotel sein wird.**

How do Peter and Henry feel when they leave Charlie at the animal center?

   a) Happy, because they know that Charlie will be happy in his hotel too.

   b) Anxious, cause Charlie never been in a hotel without them.

   c) Excited, because it will be Charlie's first experience in a hotel.

2) **Was tun sie dann als erstes?**

   a) **Sie gehen zum originalen Disney Park.**

   b) **Sie gehen zum Walt Disney Studio.**

   c) **Sie machen die gewöhnlichen Disney-Fahrten.**

What do they choose to do first?

   a) To go the Original Disney Park.

   b) To go in the Walt Disney Studio.

   c) To do the traditional Disney rides.

3) **Welchen Charakter sehen sie zuerst?**

   a) **Minnie Mouse**

   b) **Mickey Mouse**

   c) **Pluto**

Who is the first character that they see?

   a) Minnie Mouse

   b) Mickey Mouse

   c) Pluto

ANSWERS:

   1) A

   2) A

   3) C

Nach seinem Abenteuer mit Mickey und Minnie Mouse kann Henry sich nicht entscheiden, was er als nächstes tun will, also greift Peter nach einem Plan des Parks und reicht ihn ihm.

After his adventure with Mickey and Minnie Mouse, Henry can't decide what he wants to do next, so Peter picks up a plan of the park and hands it to him.

„Lass uns hinsetzen und sehen, was es da zu machen gibt. Dann können wir entscheiden, " sagt Sarah.

"Let's sit down and see exactly what there is to do. Then we can decide," says Sarah.

Henry sagt, er sei ziemlich hungrig und fragt, ob sie essen können, bevor sie etwas Weiteres machen. Gute Idee.

Henry says he's rather hungry so asks if they can eat before they do anything else. Good idea.

Den Plan benutzend, sehen sie nach den verschiedenen Restaurants und Henry verkündet, dass er Pommes Frites will. Es ist ihm egal, was er zu den Pommes Frites bekommt, aber er will Pommes Frites. Sie wählen ein Restaurant, wo Henry einen Burger mit Pommes Frites und Sarah und Peter ein Huhn mit Salat essen können.

Using the plan, they look at the different restaurants and Henry declares that he wants chips. He doesn't mind what he has with his chips, but he wants chips. They select a restaurant where Henry can have a burger with chips and Sarah and Peter can have chicken and salad.

Als sie ihr Essen gekauft haben, setzten sie sich hin und essen und schauen auf den Park-Plan. Das Essen ist nicht französische Haute-Küche, aber es ist sehr gut. Sie wissen, dass sie sich für die Fahrgeschäfte anstellen werden müssen, da es so voll ist, aber sie merken, dass sie nahe an einigen guten Fahrten sind und sind sich einig, zuerst Peter Pan zu versuchen. Als sie mit dem Essen fertig sind, gehen sie zur Peter Pan-Fahrt rüber und warten auf ihre Runde.

When they have bought their food, they sit down and eat, and look at the park plan. The food isn't French haute cuisine but it's perfectly fine. They know they will have to queue for the rides as it is so busy, but they realise that they are near to some good rides and so agree to try Peter Pan first. When they finish eating, they walk over to the Peter Pan ride and wait for their turn.

Als sie ihrer Fahrt beitreten und ihre Sitze einnehmen, ist Henry sehr aufgeregt, aber innerhalb von wenigen Sekunden schläft er ein, gegen Sarah gelehnt und verpasst den Rest der Fahrt. Sarah und Peter beschließen, es ist Zeit zurück zu dem Hotel zu gehen und etwas Schlaf zu bekommen, so dass sie genügend Energie für den nächsten Tag haben. Es wird ein langer Tag mit viel Laufen und einer Menge an Aufregung sein, so stimmen sie alle überein, dass sie alle einen gute Nacht – Schlaf benötigen.

When they join the ride and take their seat, Henry is very excited but within just a few seconds, he falls asleep, leaning against Sarah, and misses the rest of the ride. Sarah and Peter decide it's time to go back to the hotel and get some sleep so that they have enough energy for the next day. It will be a long day with lots of walking and lots of excitement, so they agree that they all need a good night's sleep.

Peter trägt Henry zur Bushaltestelle, dann erwischen sie den Bus zurück zu ihrem Hotel. Sie legen Henry ins Bett, ohne ihn aufzuwecken und setzten sich selbst hin, um alles aufzunehmen. Sie schauen auf den Plan der Parks und versuchen zu entscheiden, wo sie morgen beginnen, aber dann geben sie zu, dass sie zu müde sind und gehen selbst ins Bett.

Peter carries Henry to the bus stop, then they catch the bus back to their hotel. They put Henry to bed without him waking up and sit down themselves to take it all in. They look at the plan of the parks to try to decide where to start tomorrow, but then agree they are too tired, and head to bed themselves.

Difficult Words

1- Hungrig – Hungry

2- Es macht ihm nichts aus – He doesn't mind

3- Pommes – Chips

4- Hähnchen – Chicken

5- Gehobene Küche – Haute cuisine

6- Einwandfrei – Perfectly fine

7- Probieren – To try

8- Lernen – Leaning

9- Gegen – Against

10- Trägt – Carries

11- Morgen – Tomorrow

12- Bemerken – Realise

13- Verpasst – Misses

14- Nichts anderes – Anything else

15- Runde – Turn

Zusammenfassung der Geschichte:

Es ist immernoch erster Tag in Disneyland Paris für die Familie von Sarah und Peter. Nachdem sie mit Mickey und Minnie-Maus gesprochen haben, muss die Familie Entscheidungen treffen, welche Aktivitäten sie während des restlichen Tags unternehmen möchte.

Summary of the Story:

It's still the first day at Disneyland Paris for the family of Sarah and Peter. After talking with Mickey and Minnie Mouse, the family must make decisions about what activities to do during the rest of the day.

Quiz:

1) Wie ist ihre erste Mahlzeit in Disneyland Paris?

a) Das Essen ist nicht gehobene Küche, aber gut genug.

b) Das Essen ist gehobene Küche und ausgezeichnet.

c) Das Essen ist nicht gehobene Küche und nicht sehr gut.

How is their first meal at Disneyland Paris?

a) The food isn't haute cuisine, but it's good enough.

b) The food is haute cuisine and excellent.

c) The food isn't haute cuisine and not very good.

2) Wofür entscheiden sie sich für den nächsten Tag?

a) Sie werden zum Peter Pan-Karussell gehen.

b) Sie werden mit den Fahrgeschäften nahe des Hotels starten.

c) Sie entscheiden nichts, da sie zu müde sind.

What do they decide to do to start their next day?

a) They will go to Peter Pan ride.

b) They will start by the rides near the hotel.

c) They don't decide, because they are too tired.

3) Um diese Jahreszeit sind dort:

a) Sehr viele Leute

b) Nicht sehr viele Leute

c) So viele Leute wie normalerweise

In this time of the year, there is:

a) A lot of people

b) Not many people

c) As many people as usual

ANSWERS:

1) A

2) C

3) B

Tag zwei der Reise im Disneyland.

Day two of the trip to Disneyland.

Henry wacht, sich müde fühlend, aber sehr aufgeregt auf. Er hat Lust darauf zu frühstücken und dann in den Park zu gehen. Zum Frühstück wählt er Schokoladenmüsli gefolgt von Brot und Marmelade mit Orangensaft und heißer Schokolade zum Trinken.

Henry wakes up feeling very tired but very excited. He's keen to go to breakfast early and then into the park. For breakfast he chooses chocolate cereal followed by bread and jam, with orange juice and a hot chocolate to drink.

Sie gehen nochmals zum Park und kommentieren, dass es heute sehr heiß ist. Sie gehen wieder durch den Sicherheitsbereich und entscheiden, den Zug durch den Park zu nehmen, so können sie alles sehen, das es dort gibt. Henry ist aufgeregt, verschiedene Fahrten zu sehen und beginnt eine Liste von den Fahrten zu machen, die er machen will.

They walk to the park again and comment that it is very hot today. They go through security again, and decide to take the train around the park so that they can see everything there is to see. Henry is excited to see so many different rides and starts to make a list of the rides he wants to go to.

Sie machen zwei weitere Fahrten, bevor sie beschließen für ein Getränk zu stoppen. Sarah sagt, sie fühlt sie unwohl – sie hat Kopfschmerzen und fühlt sich übel – und sie braucht auch etwas zu essen. Sie müssen Schlange stehen und Sarah beginnt in Panik zu geraten, wird ohnmächtig und schlägt sich ihren Kopf auf dem Boden auf. Henry beginnt zu weinen und Peter geht neben Sarah auf den Boden, um mit ihr zu reden und nach ihr zu sehen. Er sieht, sie hat einen Schnitt an ihrem Kopf.

They do two more rides before deciding to stop for a drink. Sarah says she is feeling unwell – she has a headache and feels nauseous - and needs something to eat as well. They have to queue and Sarah starts to panic, faints, and hits her head on the floor. Henry starts to cry and Peter gets on to the floor next to Sarah to talk to her and check on her. He sees she has a cut on her head.

Drei Disneyland-Mitarbeiter eilen herbei, um zu helfen und bringen zwei Getränke, Limonade und Coca-Cola und animieren Sarah zu trinken, um ihrem Blutzuckerspiegel zu unterstützen.

Three Disneyland staff rush over to help, and bring two drinks, lemonade and Coca-Cola, which they encourage Sarah to drink to help her blood sugar levels.

Sie trinkt die Limonade und gibt die Coca-Cola an Henry und er hört zu weinen auf.

She drinks the lemonade and gives the Coca-Cola to Henry, and he stops crying.

Ein Mann erscheint mit einem Rollstuhl und Sarah wird zum medizinischen Zentrum gebracht, um untersucht zu werden. Der Schnitt blutet weiter, also veranlassen sie für Sarah, in das nächstgelegene Spital zu gehen, zum Röntgen und zum nähen und Peter und Henry kommen mit ihr.

A man appears with a wheelchair and Sarah is taken to the medical centre to be checked over. The cut keeps bleeding so they arrange for Sarah to go to the nearest hospital for an X-Ray and stitches, and Peter and Henry go with her.

Sie bekommt sehr schnell einen Arzt beim Spital und muss eine Menge an Tests durchlaufen, warum sie ohnmächtig wurde. Sie finden keinen Grund, außer dass sie sehr erhitzt und sehr müde ist. Sie nähen ihren Kopf und sie alle gehen zurück zum Disneyland um den Urlaub weiter fort zu führen.

She sees a doctor at the hospital very quickly and has lots of tests to check why she fainted. They do not find a reason, other than her being very hot and very tired. They stitch her head and then they all go back to Disneyland to continue their holiday.

Die Disneyland-Mitarbeiter sind sehr fürsorglich und besorgt um Sarah und bieten ihnen eine kostenlose Mahlzeit an, als sie im Park zurück sind. Sie nehmen dankbar an, da sie ziemlich hungrig sind.

The Disneyland staff are very caring and worried about Sarah and offer them a free meal when they are back in the park. They accept gratefully as they are rather hungry.

Difficult Words

1- Heiß – Hot

2- Panik – Panic

3- Kopfschmerzen – Headache

4- übel – Nauseous

5- Ohnmächtig werden – Faints

6- Schlägt – Hits

7- Weinen – To cry

8- Sprechen – To talk

9- Schnitt – Cut

10-Angestellte – Staff

11- Herbei eilen – Rush over

12-Bringen – Bring

13-Blut – Blood

14-Rollstuhl – Wheelchair

15-Stiche – Stitches

Zusammenfassung der Geschichte:

Am zweiten Tag in Disneyland Paris ist das Wetter warm und herrlich, und Henry ist sehr aufgeregt, den Tag zu starten. Aber etwas verläuft nicht so wie geplant.

Summary of the Story:

This is the second day at Disneyland Paris, the weather is warm and beautiful, and Henry is very excited to start his day. However, something is not going as planned.

Quiz:

1) Wer bemerkt die Schnittwunde an Sarahs Kopf zuerst?
  a) Henry

  b) Der Doktor

  c) Peter

Who first notices the cut on Sarah's head?
  a) Henry

  b) The doctor

  c) Peter

2) Wie reagiert Henry, als Sarah ohnmächtig wird?
  a) Er weint

  b) Er gerät in Panik

  c) Er bleibt ruhig und fragt um Hilfe.

How does Henry react when Sarah passes out?
  a) He cries

  b) He panics

  c) He stays calm and ask for help.

3) Was bringen die Angestellten Sarah, damit sie sich besser fühlt?
  a) Schokolade

  b) Energy Drinks

  c) Limonade und Coca Cola

What do the employees bring to Sarah to make her feel better?
  a) Chocolate

  b) An energy drinks

  c) A lemonade and a Coca Cola

ANSWERS:
  1) C

  2) A

  3) C

GESCHICHTE 21: NACH HAUSE KOMMEN
STORY 21: GETTING HOME

Peter, Sarah und Henry packen ihre Taschen, checken aus dem Hotel Cheyenne aus, dann gehen sie und holen Charlie. Sie gehen zurück zu ihrem Auto und beginnen, nach ihrem fantastischen und ereignisreichen Ausflug ins Disneyworld Paris nach Hause zu fahren.

Peter, Sarah and Henry pack their bags, check out of the Hotel Cheyenne, then go and collect Charlie. They walk back to their car and begin to head for home after their fantastic and eventful trip to Disneyland Paris.

Sie sind nicht sicher, welchen Weg sie für die kürzeste Reise nach Hause nehmen sollen. sie müssen Satelliten-Navigation (das Navi) benutzen, dass ihnen beim Fahren durch Paris und den richtigen Weg nach Hause zu finden hilft. Peter gibt die Koordinaten ihrer Adresse ein und sie warten auf ihre Richtung.

They aren't sure which way to go for the shortest journey home. They need to use satellite navigation (Sat Nav) to help them drive around Paris and to find the right way home. Peter sets the co-ordinates for their address and they wait for their directions.

Das Navi benötigt etwas Zeit, um die beste Route heraus zu finden.

Sat Nav spends a little time working out the best route.

Dann sagt das Navi:

Then Sat Nav says:

- **Die Wegbegleitung beginnt, sobald Sie die markierte Route befahren.**
- The guidance will start when you join the highlighted route.
- **Sobald sie die Hauptstraße erreichen, befahren Sie den Kreisverkehr und nehmen Sie die dritte Abfahrt.**
- When you reach the main road, enter the roundabout and take the third exit.
- **Fahren Sie auf der Autobahn weiter 10km gerade aus.**
- Continue straight on the motorway for 10 kms.
- **In 500 Metern biegen Sie bei der nächsten Kreuzung rechts ab.**
- In 500 metres, at the next junction, keep right.
- **Nach 150 Metern halten Sie sich rechts und fahren auf die Autobahn.**
- After 150 metres, keep right and join the motorway.
- **Fahren Sie für 5km gerade aus.**

- Continue straight for 5 kms.
- **Befahren Sie den Kreisverkehr und nehmen Sie die zweite Ausfahrt.**
- Join the roundabout and take the second exit.
- **In 1km halten Sie sich links.**
- In 1 km, keep left.
- **Befahren Sie die Autobahn.**
- Join the motorway.
- **Bleiben Sie für 100km auf der Autobahn.**
- Stay on the motorway for 100 kms.
- **Sie nähern sich einer Mautstelle. Fahren Sie langsamer und halten Sie Ihr Ticket bereit.**
- You are approaching a toll booth. Slow down and have your ticket ready.
- **Nach der Mautstelle, halten Sie sich links.**
- After the toll, keep left.
- **Halten Sie sich links.**
- Keep left.
- **Fahren Sie für 102km gerade aus.**
- Continue straight for 102 kms.
- **In 800 Metern nehmen Sie die Ausfahrt.**
- In 800 metres, take the exit.
- **Sobald Sie die Autobahn verlassen, halten Sie sich links.**
- As you leave the motorway, keep left.
- **Bei der nächsten Ausfahrt halten Sie sich rechts und folgen der Straße für 2km.**
- At the next exit, keep right and follow the road for 2 kms.
- **Sie haben Ihr Ziel erreicht –**
- You have reached your destination-

Sobald sie den Kanaltunnel erreichen, wählen sie eine Mautstelle und nähern sich dieser.

As they approach the Channel Tunnel, they select a toll booth to approach.

Sarah und Peter haben vorgebucht und wählen die automatische Mautstelle. Sie kamen früh an und sind zufrieden zu sehen, dass sie den früheren Zug durch den Tunnel nehmen können.

Sarah and Peter have pre-booked and select the automated booth. They have arrived early and are pleased to see that they can take an earlier train through the Tunnel.

Sie warten im Terminal bis ihr Buchstabencode verkündet wird und kaufen einige Sandwiches zum Mittag, während sie warten.

They wait in the terminal for their letter code to be announced, and buy some sandwiches for lunch while they are waiting.

Nach 15 Minuten wird ihr Buchstabencode aufgerufen und sie gehen zurück zu ihrem Auto, um zum Zug zu fahren und nach Hause zurück zu kehren.

After 15 minutes, their letter code is called and they walk back to their car to drive to the train and the return home.

Difficult Words

1- Ereignisreich – Eventful

2- Weg – Way

3- Benutzen – To use

4- Finden – To find

5- Koordinaten – Co-ordinates

6- Hervorgehoben – Highlighted

7- Kreisel – Roundabout

8- Ausfahrt – Exit

9- Langsamer fahren – Slow down

10-Links – Left

11- Rechts – Right

12-Zweite – Second

13-Geradeaus – Straight

14-Autobahn – Motorway

15-Bleiben – Stay

Zusammenfassung der Geschichte:

Peter, Sarah und Henry haben ihren fantastischen Urlaub in Disneyland Paris beendet und fahren nun nach Hause. Sie bereiten die Rückfahrt vor und befolgen die Anweisungen ihres Navigationssystems sorgfältig, um zurück zu finden.

Summary of the Story:

Peter, Sarah and Henry have finished their fantastic vacation at Disneyland Paris and are now ready to head home. They therefore prepare for the return trip and listen carefully to the GPS to find their way back.

Quiz:

1) Wie viele Kilometer sind es vom Kreisel bis zur Mautstation?

   a) 10 km

   b) 100 km

   c) 102 km

There are how many kilometers between the roundabout and the toll booth?

   a) 10 km

   b) 100 km

   c) 102 km

2) Sarah und Peter erreichen den Eurotunnel

   a) spät

   b) vorher

   c) gerade rechtzeitig für ihren Zug

Sarah and Peter arrive at the Channel Tunnel

   a) Late

   b) In advance

   c) Just in time for their train

3) Was kaufen sie, während sie darauf warten, dass ihr Code aufgerufen wird?

   a) Spiele, um die Zeit zu überbrücken

   b) Getränke

   c) Sandwiches

What are they buying while waiting for their letter code to be announced?

   a) Games to pass the time

   b) Drinks

   c) Sandwiches

ANSWERS:

   1) B

   2) B

   3) C

Sarah fühlt sich nach ihrem Problem in Disneyland Paris besser.

Sarah is feeling better after her problem at Disneyland Paris.

Bevor sie zurück zur Arbeit geht, vereinbart sie eine Freundin – Natalie -zum Mittagessen zu treffen.

Before she goes back to work, she arranges to meet a friend – Natalie - for lunch.

Sie treffen sich am Freitag in der Stadt und gehen, bevor sie Mittag essen, einkaufen.

They meet in town on Friday and go shopping before having lunch.

Sarah entscheidet, dass sie einige neue Kleidungsstücke für die Arbeit braucht: einen Anzug, ein hübsches Shirt, ein Kleid und definitiv neue Schuhe.

Sarah decides she needs some new clothes for work: a suit, a smart shirt, a dress, and definitely some new shoes.

Zuerst gehen sie in ein großes Kaufhaus und beginnen nach geeigneten Kleidungsstücken in der Damenbekleidungs-Abteilung zu suchen.

They go first into a large department store and start looking for suitable clothes in the ladies' clothes departments.

Sarah geht langsam herum, aber sie sieht nichts, was sie mag. Natalie macht einige Vorschläge, aber Sarah ist trotzdem nicht interessiert. Plötzlich sieht sie ein blaues Kleid, dass sie mag und probiert es an. Sie sagt, es ist zu groß und fragt nach einer kleineren Größe. Sie fragt außerdem, ob es in grün verfügbar ist. Grün ist ihre Lieblingsfarbe. Es ist in grün nicht verfügbar, nur in blau.

Sarah walks around slowly but sees nothing she likes. Natalie makes some suggestions but still Sarah is not interested. Suddenly, she sees a blue dress that she likes, and tries it on. She says it is too big and she asks for a smaller size. She also asks if it is available in green. Green is her favourite colour. It is not available in green, only in blue.

Sie probiert die kleinere Größe an und es fühlt sich zu klein an, also sucht sie weiter.

She tries the smaller size and it feels too small so she keeps looking.

Sie sieht ein weiteres Kleid in marineblau und probiert es an. Dieses Mal ist es zu klein, also fragt sie nach einer größeren Größe, die verfügbar ist und probiert dieses an. Es passt perfekt und Natalie sagt, dass es großartig aussieht, also beschließt Sarah, es zu kaufen. Natalie beschließt, das blaue Kleid von zuvor anzuprobieren und es passt ihr perfekt, also entscheidet sie sich, es für sich zu kaufen.

She sees another dress in navy blue and tries it on. This time it is too small, so she asks for a larger size, which is available, then tries that on. It fits perfectly and Natalie says it looks great, so Sarah decides to buy it. Natalie decides to try on the blue dress from earlier and it fits her perfectly, so she decides to buy that for herself.

Sarah und Natalie gehen in unzählige, verschiedene Kaufhäuser, um nach geeigneten Anzügen zu suchen. Sarah kann sich nicht entscheiden, welche Farbe sie will. Sie will sich klug fühlen, aber sie will den Anzug mit verschiedenen Tops oder Shirts anziehen. Natalie schlägt vor, sie solle nach einem grauen Anzug suchen, und sagt, dass grau sehr vielseitig ist und mit jeder Farbe geht.

Sarah and Natalie go to a number of different departments to look for a suitable suit. Sarah can't decide what colour she wants. She wants to feel smart but wants to wear the suit with a number of different tops or shirts. Natalie suggests she look for a grey suit, saying grey is very versatile and goes with any colour.

Sarah erkennt sofort einen grauen Rock, denn sie mag und sie sucht nach einer Jacke in ihrer Größe, die dazu passt. Der Verkäufer sagt, sie haben keine Jacken, die zu diesem Rock passen und schlägt einen anderen Rock vor, den Sarah mag, aber nicht so sehr.

Sarah immediately spots a grey skirt she likes and looks for a jacket in her size to go with it. The shop assistant says they do not have a jacket that goes with that skirt, and suggests a different skirt which Sarah likes, but not as much.

Sarah ist enttäuscht und fragt Natalie, „ Bist du schon fürs Mittagessen bereit? Ich verhungere!"

Sarah is disappointed and asks Natalie, "Are you ready for lunch yet? I'm starving!"

Natalie ist glücklich, Mittagessen zu gehen und sie beginnen darüber zu reden, wohin sie gehen.

Natalie is happy to go for lunch and they start to talk about where to go.

Difficult Words

1- Freitag – Friday

2- Kleidung – Clothes

3- Ein elegantes Shirt – A smart shirt

4- Ein Kleid – A dress

5- Schuhe – Shoes

6- Ein großes Kaufhaus – Large department store

7- Größe – Size

8- Kleiner – Smaller

9- Verfügbar – Available

10- Vielseitig – Versatile

11- Rock – Skirt

12- Jacket – Jacket

13- Enttäuscht – Disappointed

14- Bereit – Ready

15- Grün – Green

Zusammenfassung der Geschichte:

Sarah ist aus dem Urlaub zurück. Bevor sie zur Arbeit zurückkehrt, trifft sie sich mit ihrer Freundin Natalie und beschließt, einen Shoppingtag mit ihr zu machen, um neue Arbeitskleidung zu kaufen.

Summary of the Story:

Sarah is back from vacation, but before returning to work, she sees her friend Natalie and decides to do a shopping day with her to buy new work clothes.

Quiz:

1) Zur Mittagszeit hat Sarah gekauft:

    a) Einen grauen Rock und ein blaues Kleid.

    b) Einen grauen Anzug und einen grauen Rock.

    c) Ein blaues Kleid.

At lunch time Sarah bought:

    a) A grey skirt and a blue dress.

    b) A grey suit and grey skirt.

    c) A blue dress.

2) Wie fühlt sich Sarah, bevor sie zum Mittagessen gehen?

    a) Sie ist glücklich mit ihren Einkäufen.

    b) Enttäuscht, dass sie keine Jacke gefunden hat, die zu einem Rock passt, der ihr gefiel.

    c) Verärgert, dass sie nicht alles gefunden hat, was sie wollte.

How does Sarah feel before going for lunch?

    a) Really happy with her purchases.

    b) Disappointed for not having found a jacket matching a skirt that she likes.

    c) Angry that she couldn't find everything she wanted.

3) Warum kann sich Sarah nicht für eine Farbe für einen Anzug entscheiden?

    a) Weil sie sich modisch fühlen möchte, aber den Anzug mit verschiedenen Tops und Shirts tragen möchte.

    b) Weil sie nicht weiß, welche Farbe ihr steht.

    c) Weil sie noch nicht weiß, welche Farbe ihre Schuhe sein werden.

Why does Sarah can't decide on the color of the suit she would like?

    a) Because she wants to feel smart but wants to wear the suit with a number of different tops or shirts.

    b) Because she doesn't know what color suits her

    c) Because she doesn't know yet the color her shoes will be.

ANSWERS:

    1) C

    2) B

    3) A

Sarah und Natalie sind sich einig, Mittagessen zu gehen und beginnen darüber zu reden, wohin sie gehen.

Sarah and Natalie agree to go for lunch and start to talk about where to go.

„Ich bin ziemlich hungrig", sagt Sarah. „Würdest du italienisches Essen mögen? Eine Pizza oder vielleicht eine Pasta?"

"I'm rather hungry," says Sarah. "Would you like some Italian food? A pizza or some pasta perhaps?"

Natalie ist sich nicht sicher. „Ich bin mir nicht sicher, ob ich italienisches Essen möchte. Wie ist es mit einer chinesischen Mahlzeit irgendwo? Würde das in Ordnung sein?"

Natalie is not sure. "I'm not sure I want Italian food. How about a Chinese meal somewhere? Would that be OK?"

Sarah ist enttäuscht und schlägt einen Burger mit Pommes Frites als einen Kompromiss vor. „Würdest du stattdessen gerne einen Burger haben?", fragt sie.

Sarah is disappointed and suggests a burger and chips as a compromise. "Would you like to have a burger instead?" she asks.

„Mmmm. Ich bin mir nicht sicher, ob ich möchte," antwortet Natalie. „Ich mag die Idee von Pommes Frites, aber nicht den Burger."

"Mmmm. I'm not sure I do," answers Natalie. "I like the idea of chips but not the burger."

Beide denken für einen Moment in Ruhe nach.

They both think silently for a while.

„Was ist dann mit Fisch und Pommes Frites?", fragt Sarah.

"What about fish and chips then?" asks Sarah.

„Ja!", sagt Natalie. „Perfekt!"

"Yes!" says Natalie. "Perfect!"

Sie gehen zur Fisch und Pommes Frites - Bar und bestellen ihr Mittagessen. Beide fragen nach extra Salz, Essig und Mayonnaise, sowie nach Brot und Butter dazu. Was für ein perfektes Mittagessen!

They go to the fish and chip bar and order their lunch. They both ask for extra salt and vinegar, and mayonnaise, as well as bread and butter to go with it. What a perfect lunch!

Sie trinken Tee zu ihren Fisch mit Pommes Frites und reden über das Einkaufen.

They drink tea with their fish and chips and chat about their shopping.

Sarah sagt, sie sei enttäuscht, nicht den passenden Anzug gefunden zu haben. Natalie schlägt vor, zurück zum Kaufhaus zu gehen, um den Anzug anzuprobieren, den der Verkäufer vorschlug, aber Sarah sagt, sie wolle wo anders schauen.

Sarah says she's disappointed not to have found the right suit. Natalie suggests she go back to the department store to try on the suit the shop assistant suggested but Sarah says she wants to look somewhere else.

Sie beschließen nach dem Mittagessen in einen anderen Shop zu gehen.

They agree to go to a different shop after lunch.

Sie gehen gemeinsam hinein und sofort sieht Sarah einen grauen Anzug, denn sie mag. Sie fragt danach, ihn anzuprobieren.

They walk in together and, immediately, Sarah sees a grey suit that she likes. She asks to try it on.

Der Verkäufer findet den Anzug in Sarahs Größe und Sarah probiert ihn an. Sie verlässt die Umkleidekabine und Natalie sagt, „Wow!", gefolgt von, „Das passt dir perfekt und sieht fantastisch aus"!.

The shop assistant finds the suit in Sarah's size and Sarah tries it on. She walks out of the changing room and Natalie says, "Wow!", followed by, "That fits you perfectly and looks fantastic!".

Sarah ist so erleichtert und lächelt. Sie beschließt, ihn zu kaufen und nimmt ihre Kreditkarte aus ihrer Geldbörse, um zu bezahlen. Sie fragt den Verkäufer, „Wie viel macht das?". Sie ist überrascht und erfreut zu erfahren, dass der Anzug im Abverkauf ist und nur €150 kostet.

Sarah is so relieved and smiles. She decides to buy it and takes her credit card from her purse to pay. She asks the assistant, "How much is that?". She is surprised and pleased to learn the suit is in the sale and only costs €150.

Was für ein Schnäppchen!

What a bargain!

Difficult Words

1- Nudeln – Pasta

2- Fisch – Fish

3- Extra – Extra

4- Essig – Vinegar

5- Shop-Assistentin – Shop assistant

6- Woanders – Somewhere else

7- Sofort – Immediately

8- Umkleidekabine – Changing room

9- Erleichtert – Relieved

10- Geldbörse – Purse

11- Erfreut – Pleased

12- Kreditkarte – Credit card

13- Grau – Grey

14- Ein Anzug – A suit

15- Wie viel – How much

Zusammenfassung der Geschichte:

Sarah und Natalie setzen ihren Einkaufstag fort, legen jedoch erst einen Mittagessenstopp ein. Wird Sarah finden, was sie braucht?

Summary of the Story:

Sarah and Natalie continue their shopping day, but stop first to eat their lunch. Will Sarah find everything she needs?

Quiz:

1) Wie reagiert Sarah, als sie den Preis des Anzugs erfährt?

   a) Sie ist enttäuscht, weil er teurer als gedacht ist.

   b) Sie ist erstaunt und erfreut, da er günstiger als angenommen ist.

   c) Sie reagiert gar nicht, weil sie der Preis nicht interessiert.

What is Sarah's reaction when learning the price of the suit?

   a) She is disappointed, because it is more expensive than she thought.

   b) She is surprised and pleased because it is cheaper than she thought.

   c) She doesn't have a reaction, because she doesn't care about the price.

2) Was tut Sarah, als Natalie vorschlägt, chinesisch zu essen?

   a) Sie akzeptiert die Idee.

   b) Sie ist enttäuscht und schlägt vor, alleine zu essen.

   c) Sie schlägt stattdessen Hamburger und Pommes Frites vor.

What does Sarah do when Natalie offers her to eat Chinese?

   a) She accepts her idea.

   b) She is disappointed and suggests eating alone.

   c) She suggests eating a hamburger and fries instead.

3) Was schlägt Natalie vor, als Sarah ihr erzählt, dass sie enttäuscht ist, keinen Anzug gefunden zu haben?

   a) Sie schlägt vor, in einem anderen Laden Ausschau zu halten

   b) Sie schlägt vor, zum vorigen Geschäft zurückzugehen und den Anzug anzuprobieren, den die Assistentin vorgeschlagen hat.

   c) Sie schlägt vor, an einem anderen Tag zu gucken, wenn es mehr Sonderangebote gibt.

What does Nathalie offer when Sarah tells her that she is disappointed not to have found a suit?

   a) She suggests changing store and keep looking.

   b) She suggests going back to the previous store to try on the suit the shop assistant suggested.

   c) She suggests continuing to look another day when there will have more discount choices.

ANSWERS:

   1) B

   2) C

   3) B

Sarah fühlt sich gut bei ihren Einkaufs-Ausflug und beginnt über ihr Shirt und die Schuhe, die sie will, nachzudenken.

Sarah is feeling good about her shopping trip now and starts to think about her shirt and the shoes she wants.

Sarah und Natalie gehen zurück zum Kaufhaus, um nach Damen-Shirts zu suchen und entdecken, dass es dort eine riesige Auswahl in einer Vielzahl von Abteilungen gibt.

Sarah and Natalie go back to the department store to look for ladies' shirts and find there is a huge choice in a number of departments.

Sarah ist begeistert darüber, wie viele es zum Auswählen gibt und beschließt, zwei Shirts zu kaufen, die zu ihem grauen Anzug passen.

Sarah is amazed how many there are to choose from and decides she will buy two shirts to go with her grey suit.

Zuerst sucht sie nach einem weißen Shirt. Einfach und klassisch. Sie findet drei und probiert sie an. Eines ist zu groß, eines ist zu klein und eines passt gut, außer dass die Ärmel zu lange sind. Sie sucht weiter.

First, she looks for a white shirt. Simple and classic. She finds three and tries them on. One is too big, one is too small, and one fits well except the sleeves are too long. She continues looking.

Sie findet zwei weitere, kann aber ihre Größe in keinem von beiden entdecken. Sie fragt die Verkäuferin, ob sie ihre Größe haben und diese geht weg, um danach zu suchen. Sie kommt glücklich zurück und Sarah probiert die beiden Shirts an.

She finds two more but can't find her size in one of them. She asks the shop assistant if they have her size and she goes away to find it. She comes back happy, and Sarah tries on the two shirts.

Dieses Mal passen beide perfekt und sie hat eine schwierige Entscheidung zu treffen. Ach je! Sarah zeigt beide Shirts Natalie und gerade heraus sagt Natalie, welches sie kaufen soll.

This time, they are both perfect and she has a difficult decision to make. Oh dear! Sarah shows both shirts to Natalie and, straightaway, Natalie tells her which one to buy.

Sarah stimmt zu und sucht dann ein weiteres Shirt in einer anderen Farbe. Sie findet dasselbe Shirt in rosa und sie ist erfreut. Also kauft Sarah 2 Shirts desselben Styles, eines in Weiß und eines in Rosa.

Sarah agrees and then looks for another shirt in a different colour. She finds the same shirt in pink and she is delighted. So, Sarah buys 2 shirts the same style, one in white and one in pink.

Natalie erinnert sie, dass sie ebenso nach Schuhen suchen und sie gehen zum Schuh-Kaufhaus.

Natalie reminds her that they are also looking for shoes, and they head for the shoe department.

Sarah entscheidet, nach feinen, schwarzen Schuhen zu suchen und Natalie fügt hinzu, dass sie marineblaue Schuhe für die Arbeit möchte.

Sarah decides to look for some smart black shoes, and Natalie adds that she wants some navy blue shoes for work.

Beide sehen sofort schicke Lederschuhe, welche, so scheint es, in marineblau und schwarz verfügbar sind. Sie fragen den Verkäufer nach ihren Größen – Sarah hat 39 und Natalie hat 37 – und zu deren Überraschung hat der Shop beide Größen in beiden Farben.

They both immediately see some smart leather shoes which seem to be available in both navy blue and black. They ask the assistant for their size – Sarah is a 39 and Natalie is a 37 – and to their surprise, the shop has both sizes in both colours.

Sie probieren diese an, gehen im Kaufhaus für einen kurzen Augenblick herum und beschließen dann, sie zu kaufen.

They try them on, walk around the department for a short while, then decide to buy them.

Sarah geht nach einem sehr erfolgreichen Einkaufstag nach Hause und hat viel Geld ausgegeben. Na gut...

Sarah goes home having had a very successful shopping day and having spent a great deal of money. Oh well...

Difficult Words

1- Zurückgehen – Go back

2- Abteilungen – Departments

3- Erstaunt – Amazed

4- Weiß – White

5- Ärmel – Sleeves

6- Dieses Mal – This time

7- Gott – God

8- Pink – Pink

9- Schwarz – Black

10- Marineblau – Navy

11- Leder – Leather

12- Erfolgreich – Successful

13- Geld – Money

14- Nach – After

15- Ein Tag – A day

Zusammenfassung der Geschichte:

Sarah genießt nun ihren Einkaufstag, und sie findet mehr und mehr Kleidungsstücke, nach denen sie gesucht hat. Es gibt jedoch noch ein paar Dinge, die sie finden muss.

Summary of the Story:

Sarah is now enjoying her shopping day as she finds more and more items that she is looking for. However, she still has several other things she needs to find.

Quiz:

1) Welche Farbe haben die Schuhe, die Natalie kaufen möchte?

    a) Schwarz

    b) Pink

    c) Marineblau

What color are the shoes that Natalie wants to buy?

    a) Black

    b) Pink

    c) Navy blue

2) Welche Schuhgröße hat Sarah?

    a) 39

    b) 37

    c) 38

What is Sarah's shoes size?

    a) 39

    b) 37

    c) 38

3) Wer kauft Schuhe?

    a) Sarah

    b) Natalie

    c) Sarah und Natalie

Who buys shoes?

    a) Sarah

    b) Natalie

    c) Sarah et Natalie

ANSWERS:

    1) C

    2) A

    3) C

Es ist die letzte Woche der Ferien und Peter fragt Henry, was er gerne machen würde.

It is the last week of the holidays and Peter asks Henry what he would like to do.

Jede Woche geht Henry in ein Sommercamp in einem lokalen Sportcenter und er sagt, er will das noch immer machen, da er gewöhnlich seine Freunde dort trifft.

Every week, Henry goes to the summer camp in the local sports centre and he says he still wants to do that as usual as he meets his friends there.

Peter ist damit zufrieden und stimmt zu. Dann macht er einige Vorschläge für die weiteren Tage.

Peter is pleased about that and agrees. Then he makes some suggestions for the other days.

„Gut, wir müssen an einem Tag eine neue Schuluniform kaufen, ich weiß das," sagt Peter.

"Well, we need to buy you some new school uniform one day, I know that," says Peter.

Henry fragt, „Können wir an einem Tag etwas backen, Papa? Wir haben seit Jahren nichts gebacken."

Henry asks, "Can we do some baking one day, Dad? We haven't done baking for ages."

Du hast recht, haben wir nicht," stimmt Peter zu. „ Wir könnten einen Schokoladenkuchen machen und vielleicht Scones? Aber wir müssen nochmals einige Hausarbeiten machen und das Haus und den Garten ordentlich und sauber hinterlassen.

"You're right, we haven't," agrees Peter. "We could make a chocolate cake and perhaps some scones? But we need to do some housework again and leave the house, and garden, neat and tidy."

Henry weiß, er wird dabei helfen und hofft, dass er am Ende eine Belohnung bekommt. Aber er weiß auch, dass es nicht so sein könnte, da er jede Woche Taschengeld bekommt.

Henry knows he will help with this and hopes he will get a treat at the end. But he also knows he may not because he has pocket money every week.

„Lass uns damit beginnen, das wir mit Charlie rausgehen, oder?" schlägt Peter Henry vor.

"Let's start by taking Charlie for a walk, shall we?" Peter suggests to Henry.

„Können wir dann zum Park gehen, Papa?" fragt Henry. Henry liebt es, einen Ball zum Park mitzunehmen und ihn für Charlie zu werfen, um ihn danach zu rennen und ihn zurück zu bringen.

"Can we go to the park then, Dad?" asks Henry. Henry loves taking a ball to the park and throwing it for Charlie to run after and bring back.

Henry geht nach oben, um seine Turnschuhe für das Spazieren und Spielen im Park anzuziehen und Peter holt Charlies Leine heraus. Charlie weiß sofort, dass sie Spazieren gehen und ist sehr aufgeregt.

Henry goes upstairs to get his trainers to wear for the walk and to play in the park, and Peter picks up Charlie's lead. Charlie knows straightaway that they're going for a walk and is vey excited.

Auf dem Weg nach draußen nehmen sie den Tennisball mit.

On the way out of the house, they pick up a tennis ball.

Es dauert 15 Minuten, um zum Park zu gelangen. Als sie dort ankommen, merken sie, dass sie die einzigen Menschen im Park sind, also haben sie eine Menge Platz zum Rennen und Spielen. Henry und Charlie sind beide sehr aufgeregt und spielen glücklich über eine Stunde, werfend, jagend, fangend, und holend.

It takes fifteen minutes to get to the park. When they get there, they find they are the only people in the park so they have lots of space to run around and play. Henry and Charlie are both very excited and play happily for more than an hour, throwing, chasing, catching, fetching.

Sie sind beide erschöpft, also sitzt Henry auf einer Schaukel und Charlie liegt in der Nähe am Boden. Sie warten ein paar Minuten, bevor sie zurückgehen.

They are both exhausted so Henry sits on a swing and Charlie lies on the ground nearby. They wait a few minutes before they walk back.

Als sie nach Hause gehen, sagt Henry, „Papa, Ich glaube, meine Turnschuhe sind nun zu klein. Können wir morgen für meine neue Schuluniform einkaufen gehen und auch Turnschuhe kaufen?"

As they are walking home, Henry says, "Dad, I think my trainers are too small now. Can we go shopping for my new school uniform tomorrow and buy some trainers as well?"

„Ja, können wir. Gute Idee," sagt Peter.

"Yes, we can. Good idea," says Peter.

Difficult Words

1- Woche – Week

2- Sommer – Summer

3- Wie gewöhnlich – As usual

4- Freunde – Friends

5- Garten – Garden

6- Aufgeräumt – Tidy

7- Hoffen – Hope

8- Taschengeld – Pocket money

9- Werfen – Throwing

10-Turnschuhe – Trainers

11- Leine – Lead

12-Jagen – Chasing

13-Fangen – Catching

14-Schaukel – Swing

15-Erschöpft – Exhausted

Zusammenfassung der Geschichte:

Es ist letzte Ferienwoche, und Peter und Henry nutzen die Gelegenheit, um mit ihrem Hund Charlie in den Park zu gehen und zu planen, wie sie die letzten Ferientage verbringen möchten.

Summary of the Story:

It's the last week of vacation and Peter and Henry take the opportunity to go to the park with their dog Charlie and plan what they will do during their last days of rest.

Quiz:

1) Was sind die Aufgaben, die sie nach dem Spaziergang im Park erledigen müssen?

    a) Scones und Schokoladenkuchen backen.

    b) Haus und Garten sauber machen.

    c) Staubsaugen und Lebensmittel einkaufen.

What are the choirs they need to do after their walk in the park?

    a) To cook scones and chocolate cake.

    b) To clean the house and the garden.

    c) To vacuum and do the grocery.

2) Wie lange bleiben sie im Park?

    a) 15 Minuten

    b) Mehr als eine Stunde

    c) Den ganzen Morgen

How long do they stay in the park?

    a) 15 minutes

    b) More than an hour

    c) All morning

3) Im Park ist/sind:

    a) Niemand

    b) Einige wenige Leute, aber viel Platz, um rumzurennen und zu spielen.

    c) Viele Menschen

In the park, there is:

    a) Nobody else

    b) Few people, but lots of space to run around and play.

    c) Lots of people

ANSWERS:

    1) B

    2) B

    3) A

Es ist die letzte Woche der Ferien. Peter und Henry haben eine Menge an Dingen zu tun.

It is the last week of the holidays. Peter and Henry have a list of things to do.

Heute ist der Tag, um eine neue Schuluniform und besonders neue Turnschuhe zu kaufen.

Today is the day for buying new school uniform and, in particular, new trainers.

Peter findet die Schuluniform-Liste und beginnt mit Henry, sie durch zu gehen. Peter sagt den Artikel und Henry findet die Schuluniform letzten Jahres und probiert sie an, um zu sehen, ob sie noch immer passt. Falls nicht, kommt sie auf die Einkaufsliste. Falls doch, gut, eine Sache weniger zu kaufen.

Peter finds the school uniform list and starts to go through it with Henry. Peter says the item, and Henry finds the uniform from last year and tries it on to see if it still fits. If it doesn't, it goes on the shopping list. If it does, good, one less thing to buy.

Peter sagt, " Lass uns die neuen Turnschuhe oben auf die Liste setzen. Wir wissen, sie sind zu klein. Und sie beginnen eine Liste.

Peter says, "Let's put new trainers at the top of the list. We know they're too small." And they start the list.

EINKAUFSLISTE:
• **Turnschuhe**
SHOPPING LIST:
• Trainers

Henry probiert seine kurzen Hosen und langen Hosen an und meint, dass die kurzen Hosen passen, aber die langen Hosen nun zu kurz sind.

Henry tries on his shorts and trousers and finds the shorts fit, but the trousers are too short now.

• **Turnschuhe**
• **2 Paar dunkelgraue, lange Hosen**
• Trainers
• 2 pairs of dark grey trousers

Dann probieren sie die Poloshirts an. Sie sind jetzt auch zu kurz und sie sehen mehr grau, als weiß aus, also fügt Peter diese auch auf die Liste hinzu.

Then they try on the polo shirts. They are also too short now, and they look grey rather than white, so Peter adds those to the list as well.

- **Turnschuhe**
- **2 Paar dunkelgraue, lange Hosen**
- **5 weiße Poloshirts**
- Trainers
- 2 pairs of dark grey trousers
- 5 white polo shirts

„Wo ist dein Sweatshirt, Henry?" fragt Peter.

"Where is your sweatshirt, Henry?" asks Peter.

„Ich konnte es am Ende des Semesters nicht finden, Papa. Ich brauche unbedingt ein Neues."

"I couldn't find it at the end of term, Dad. I definitely need a new one."

- **Turnschuhe**
- **2 Paar dunkelgraue, lange Hosen**
- **5 weiße Poloshirts**
- **Rotes Sweatshirt**
- Trainers
- 2 pairs of dark grey trousers
- 5 white polo shirts
- Red sweatshirt

„So wie die Tennisschuhe, was ist mit deinem Turnzeug? Brauchst du neue, kurze Hosen zum Turnen?" fragt Peter Henry.

"As well as trainers, what about your PE kit? Do you need any new shorts for PE?" Peter asks Henry.

„Ich werte sie probieren, antwortet Henry. Er merkt, dass sie noch passen, aber er braucht neue Turnsocken.

"I'll try them on," replies Henry. He finds that they still fit, but he needs new PE socks.

- **Turnschuhe**
- **2 Paar dunkelgraue, lange Hosen**

- **5 weiße Poloshirts**
- **Rotes Sweatshirt**
- **Weiße Turnsocken**
- Trainers
- 2 pairs of dark grey trousers
- 5 white polo shirts
- Red sweatshirt
- White PE socks

„Ich glaube, du brauchst auch neue, graue Socken, Henry, also lass uns diese auch auf die Liste setzen", schlägt Peter vor.

"I think you need new grey socks as well, Henry, so let's put those on the list as well," Peter suggests.

- **Turnschuhe**
- **2 Paar dunkelgraue, lange Hosen**
- **5 weiße Poloshirts**
- **Rotes Sweatshirt**
- **Weiße Turnsocken**
- **5 Paar graue Socken**
- Trainers
- 2 pairs of dark grey trousers
- 5 white polo shirts
- Red sweatshirt
- White PE socks
- 5 pairs of grey socks

Und schließlich denken sie an Henrys Schul-Schuhe. Henry probiert sie an und, wie seine Turnsschuhe, sind sie jetzt zu klein, also müssen sie auf die Einkaufsliste kommen.

And finally, they think about Henry's school shoes. Henry tries them on and, like his trainers, they are now too small, so they also need to go on the shopping list.

Peter suggests.
- **Turnschuhe**
- **2 Paar dunkelgraue, lange Hosen**
- **5 weiße Poloshirts**
- **Rotes Sweatshirt**

- **Weiße Turnsocken**
- **5 Paar graue Socken**
- **Schwarze Schul-Schuhe**
- Trainers
- 2 pairs of dark grey trousers
- 5 white polo shirts
- Red sweatshirt
- White PE socks
- 5 pairs of grey socks
- Black school shoes

Peter und Henry sehen auf die Liste und sind sich einig, dass sie einen beschäftigten Tag mit Einkaufen vor sich haben.

Peter and Henry both look at the list and agree they have a busy day of shopping ahead of them.

Difficult Words

1- Dinge – Things
2- Der Artikel – The item
3- Letztes Jahr – Last year
4- Weniger – Less
5- Hose – Trousers
6- Dunkel – Dark
7- Rot – Red
8- Socken – Socks
9- Schule – School
10-Voraus – Ahead
11- Sportzeug – PE kit
12-Saison – Term
13-Zu kurz – Too short
14-Lieber – Rather
15-Fügt hinzu – Adds

Zusammenfassung der Geschichte:

Heute planen Peter und Henry ihren Einkaufstag und machen eine Liste mit allem, was sie für Henrys Rückkehr zur Schule kaufen müssen.

Summary of the Story:

Today Peter and Henry are planning their shopping day and making a list of everything they need for Henry's return to school.

Quiz:

1) Wie viele weiße Poloshirts benötigen sie?

   a) 2

   b) 5

   c) 1

How many white polo shirts do they need?

   a) 2

   b) 5

   c) 1

2) Welche Farbe hat das Sweatshirt?

   a) Weiß

   b) Schwarz

   c) Rot

What color is the sweatshirt?

   a) White

   b) Black

   c) Red

3) Wie viele Socken müssen sie insgesamt kaufen?

   a) 20

   b) 10

   c) 5

In total, how many socks do they need to buy?

   a) 20

   b) 10

   c) 5

ANSWERS:

   1) B

   2) C

   3) B

Mit der Schuluniform-Einkaufsliste in der Hand, steigen Peter und Henry in das Auto und fahren in die Stadt.

With the school uniform shopping list in hand, Peter and Henry get into the car to drive to town.

Als sie ankommen, gehen sie zuerst in ein Sportgeschäft, um Turnschuhe zu kaufen. Henry probiert 4 verschiedene Paare an – ein ganz weißes Paar, ein Paar ist blau und weiß, ein Paar ist rot und schwarz und schließlich ein weißes und grünes Paar. Peter denkt, die Blauen und Weißen sehen am besten aus, aber Henry möchte die Roten und Schwarzen, weil sie ihn an sein Lieblings-Fußballteam erinnern. Sie kosten mehr, aber Peter stimmt dem roten und schwarzen Paar zu.

When they arrive, they go first to a sports shop to buy some trainers. Henry tries on 4 different pairs – one all white pair, one pair that is blue and white, one pair that is red and black, and finally a white and green pair. Peter thinks the blue and white look best but Henry wants the red and black, because they remind him of his favourite football team. They cost more, but Peter agrees to the red and black pair.

Während sie im Sportgeschäft sind, kaufen sie Henrys weiße Turnsocken.

While they are in the sports shop, they buy Henry's white PE socks.

Dann gehen sie zu einem gutbekannten Kaufhaus, um nach den fünf weiteren Produkten zu suchen, die Schuhe eingeschlossen.

They then go to a well-known department store to look for the other five items, including the shoes.

Sie finden das weiße Poloshirt sofort und sie können ebenso die fünf Shirts, die Henry benötigt, in den Einkaufskorb legen. In der Nähe der Poloshirts sind die Sweatshirts, in verschiedenen Farben: marineblau, grün, lila, gelb und dankenswerterweise, rot. Also geht ein rotes Sweatshirt in Henrys Größe in den Einkaufskorb.

They find the white polo shirts straightaway and are able to put the five shirts Henry needs into the shopping basket. Near to the polo shirts are the sweatshirts in different colours: navy blue, green, purple, yellow and, thankfully, red. So, a red sweatshirt in Henry's size goes into the shopping basket.

Die grauen Socken sind einfach zu finden – es gibt genügend in der richtigen Größe. Fünf Paare kommen in den Einkaufskorb.

The grey socks are just as easy to find – there are plenty in the right size. Five pairs go into the shopping basket.

Es gibt auch unzählige, auswählbare Hosen – so denkt Peter. Er sieht sich beinahe jedes Paar am Gestell an und findet nur ein Paar, dass die richtige Größe für Henry hat. Peter gibt diese in den Korb und versucht einen Verkäufer zu finden. Aber dann beschließt Peter sich nicht zu sorgen, da Henry für die ersten paar Wochen zurück an der Schule kurze Hosen tragen wird und sie ein Paar online bestellen und darauf warten können.

There are plenty of trousers to choose from as well – or so Peter thinks. He looks at nearly every pair on the racks and only finds one pair that are the right size for Henry. Peter puts them in the basket and tries to find an assistant. But then Peter decides not to worry as Henry will wear shorts for the first few weeks back at school, and they can order a pair online and wait for them to arrive.

Sie gehen zur Kasse und zahlen für die Artikel im Korb.

They go to the till and pay for the items in the basket.

Und nun die Schuhe. Sie gehen zur Schuh-Abteilung, wo es viele Paare zur Auswahl gibt. Einige mit Schnürsenkel, andere mit Klettverschluss. Peter beschließt, dass Schnürsenkel-Schuhe besser sind und Henry probiert ein Paar an, von denen er sagt, sie sind sehr bequem. Sie sehen auch schick aus. Also zahlt Peter ebenso für die Schuhe.

And now the shoes. They go to the shoe department where there are many pairs to choose from. Some with laces, some with Velcro straps. Peter decides that laced shoes are better and Henry tries on a pair that he says are really comfortable. They look smart as well. So, Peter pays for the shoes as well.

Mit einer Menge an Einkaufstaschen zum Tragen, schlägt Peter vor einen Kaffee trinken zu gehen, bevor sie nach Hause gehen. Henry fragt, ob er etwas zu essen haben kann, da Einkaufen ihn hungrig macht.

With lots of bags to carry, Peter suggests they go for a drink before going home. Henry asks if he can have something to eat as shopping makes him hungry.

Kaffee und Kuchen für Peter, Coca-Cola und Kuchen für Henry.

Coffee and cake for Peter, Coca-Cola and cake for Henry.

Difficult Words

1- Sportgeschäft – Sports shop
2- Gutbekannt – Well known
3- Inklusive – Including
4- Korb – Basket
5- Lila – Purple
6- Gelb – Yellow
7- Regale – Racks
8- Sich Sorgen machen – To worry
9- Wird tragen – Will wear
10- Bestellen – To order
11- Schnürsenkel – Laces
12- Klettverschluss – Velcro straps
13- Bequem – Comfortable
14- Tragen – To carry
15- Schlägt vor – Suggests

Zusammenfassung der Geschichte:

Ihre Einkaufsliste ist nun komplett, und Peter und Henry gehen zum Einkaufszentrum, um alles zu kaufen, was sie benötigen. Werden sie an einem Tag alles finden?

Summary of the Story:

Now that their shopping list is complete, Peter and Henry go to the shopping center to buy everything they need. Will they manage to find everything in one day?

Quiz:

1) Was ist der erste Artikel, den sie kaufen?
   a) Turnschuhe

   b) Socken

   c) Hosen

What is the first item that they buy?
   a) Trainers

   b) Socks

   c) Trousers

2) Wie sind die Schuhe beschaffen, die Peter und Henry kaufen?
   a) Mit Schnürsenkeln

   b) Mit Klettverschluss

   c) Mit Schnürsenkeln und Klettverschluss

How are the shoes that Peter and Henry choose?
   a) With laces

   b) With Velcro straps

   c) With laces and Velcro straps

3) Was bekommt Henry zum Essen?
   a) Einen Kaffee und Kuchen.

   b) Coca Cola und Kuchen.

   c) Limonade und einen Keks.

What does Henry buy to eat?
   a) A coffee and a cake.

   b) A Coca Cola and a cake.

   c) A lemonade and a cookie.

ANSWERS:
   1) A

   2) A

   3) B

Heute ist Henrys letzter Tag im Sommercamp im lokalen Sportcenter.

Today is Henry's last day at the Summer Camp in the local sports centre.

Als er aufwacht, packt er seine Tasche mit seiner Schwimmkleidung und Handtuch und holt seine neuen Turnschuhe heraus.

When he gets up, he packs his bag with his swimming costume and towel, and gets out his new trainers.

Er zieht seine Fußballsachen und die neuen Turnschuhe an und geht runter zum Frühstücken.

He puts on his football kit and new trainers and goes downstairs for breakfast.

Unten macht Peter für Henry bereits ein Sandwich zum Mittagessen und sie reden darüber, was Henry heute im Sommercamp machen würde.

Peter is downstairs already making Henry's sandwich for lunch, and they talk about what Henry might do today at the summer camp.

„Gut, wir spielen immer Fußball. Das ist der beste Teil. Es gibt genügend Personen für sechs Mannschaften und ein paar Auswechselspieler und wir spielen während des Tages ein Turnier. Zwischen den Spielen können wir schwimmen gehen oder wir spielen Badminton," erklärt Henry.

"Well, we always play football. That's the best part. There are enough people for six teams and a few substitutes, and we play a tournament during the day. In between games, we can go swimming, or play badminton," Henry explains.

„Es gibt auch andere Dinge zu tun, die wir auswählen können", fügt Henry hinzu.

"There are other things to do as well, we choose," Henry adds.

Nachdenklich, sagt er, „Ich denke, dass ich heute auch einige andere Aktivitäten versuchen werden, da es mein letzter Tag im Camp ist."

Thoughtfully, he says, "I think that I will try some different activities today as well, as it is my last day at camp."

„Ich mag die Idee von Bogenschießen", sagt Henry. „Was denkst du, Papa?"

"I like the idea of archery," Henry says. "What do you think, Dad?"

„Großartig. Versuche es. Es klingt nach Spaß. Und welche anderen Aktivitäten gibt es dort zu tun?" fragt Peter.

"Great. Have a go. It sounds like fun. And what other activities are there to do?" Peter asks.

Henry antwortet, " Hmmh, es gibt Kanu fahren im Schwimmbad. Obwohl ich denke, ich möchte das nicht machen. Es gibt ein Trampolin und Basketball, denke ich."

Henry replies, "Well, there's canoeing in the swimming pool. I don't think I want to do that though. There's also trampolining, and basketball, I think."

„Kannst du auch alle Aktivitäten machen, wenn du willst?" fragt Peter Henry.

"Can you do all of the activities if you want to?" Peter asks Henry.

„Ja", antwortet Henry. „Du musst sie bloß zwischen den Fußballspielen tun!"

"Yes," Henry answers, "You just have to do them between the football matches!"

Sie packen Henrys eingepacktes Mittagessen in seinen Rucksack. Henry beendet sein Frühstück und sie gehen.

They put Henry's packed lunch into his rucksack. Henry finishes his breakfast, and they leave.

Charlie sieht beim Gedanken an einen Tag mit sich alleine traurig aus.

Charlie looks sad at the thought of a day on his own.

Peter fährt zum Sportcenter, parkt und führt Henry rauf zum Anmeldeschalter. Es gibt dort viele Mitarbeiter, so wie auch eine Menge an energiegeladenen Kindern, genauso wie Henry. Sie sehen glücklich und aufgeregt aus, sich gegenseitig zu sehen und Peter weiß, dass Henry einen großartigen Tag haben wird.

Peter drives to the sports centre, parks, and takes Henry up to the registration desk. There are lots of staff there, as well as lots of energetic children, just like Henry. They look happy and excited to see each other and Peter knows that Henry is going to have a great day.

Und so wird es auch Peter!

And so is Peter!

Difficult Words

1- Letzte(r) – Last

2- Schwimmkostüm – Swimming costume

3- Handtuch – Towel

4- Packen – Packs

5- Beste(r) – Best

6- Mannschaften – Teams

7- Ersatz – Substitutes

8- Wir haben gewählt – We choose

9- Ein Turnier – A tournament

10-Bogenschießen – Archery

11- Kanufahren – Canoeing

12-Anmeldeschalter – Registration desk

13-Kinder – Children

14-Trampolin springen – Trampolining

15-Rucksack – Rucksack

Zusammenfassung der Geschichte:

Heute ist Henrys letzter Tag im Sommercamp des heimischen Sportscenters. Er ist sehr aufgeregt, denn heute ist der Tag des Fußballturniers, wo er seine Freunde sehen und neue Aktivitäten ausprobieren kann.

Summary of the Story:

Today is Henry's last day at the summer camp in the local sports center. He is very excited because it is the day of the football tournament where he can see his friends and try new activities.

Quiz:

1) Welches Outfit trägt Henry heute?

   a) Eine Sporthose mit seinen neuen Turnschuhen.

   b) Sein neues weißes Poloshirt mit seinen Sportshorts.

   c) Seine Fußball-Ausstattung und die neuen Turnschuhe.

What is Henry's outfit today?

   a) A Sport short with his new trainers.

   b) His new white polo with his sport short.

   c) His football kit and new trainers.

2) Es gibt genug Spieler, um wie viele Mannschaften zu bilden?

   a) 5

   b) 6

   c) 7

There are enough players to create how many teams?

   a) 5

   b) 6

   c) 7

3) Wo findet das Kanufahren statt?

   a) Im Fluss neben dem Fußballfeld.

   b) Im See neben dem Fußballfeld.

   c) Im Swimmingpool.

Where is located the canoeing activity?

   a) In the river near the football field.

   b) In the lake near the football field.

   c) In the swimming pool.

ANSWERS:

   1) C

   2) B

   3) C

Henry ist im Sommercamp und heute ist der letzte Tag der Ferien, an dem Peter tun kann, was auch immer er will, bevor er nächste Woche als Lehrer zurück zur Arbeit geht.

Henry is at summer camp and today is the last day of the holidays when Peter can do whatever he wants to do before he goes back to work as a teacher next week.

Peter macht mit Charlie einen langen Spaziergang. Sie gehen in den Park und gehen durch die Felder und kommen nach acht Kilometern zu Hause an. Charlie legt sich für einen langen Schlaf hin.

Peter takes Charlie for a long walk. They go to the park and then walk through the fields and arrive home after eight kilometres. Charlie lies down for a long sleep.

Peter geht in die Küche, um ein frühes Mittagessen vorzubereiten und fängt an, darüber nachzudenken, was er wirklich am Nachmittag machen will.

Peter goes into the kitchen to prepare an early lunch and stops to think about what he really wants to do during the afternoon.

Was sind seine Optionen?

What are his options?

Er kann zu Hause bleiben und fernsehen. Nein, er könnte das tun, wann auch immer er will.

He can stay at home and watch TV. No, he can do that whenever he wants to.

Er könnte einkaufen gehen, um Lebensmittel für die nächste Woche zu kaufen. Nein, er kann, wann immer er will, online Lebensmittel einkaufen.

He can go shopping to buy food for next week. No, he can shop online for food whenever he wants to.

Er könnte eine Runde Golf spielen gehen. Nein, er würde lieber Begleitung haben, um dies zu tun, er mag es nicht, alleine zu spielen.

He can go and play a round of golf. No, he would rather have company to do that, he doesn't like playing on his own.

Er könnte schwimmen gehen. Nein, er will noch nicht zum Sportcenter zurückgehen.

He can go for a swim. No, he doesn't want to go back to the sports centre yet.

Er könnte den Rasen mähen, das Haus reinigen, das Auto waschen und die Badezimmer sauber machen. Nein, er wird das morgen mit Henrys Hilfe machen. Das wird mehr Spaß machen.

He can mow the lawn, clean the house, wash the car, and clean the bathrooms. No, he will do that tomorrow with Henry's help. That will be more fun.

Er könnte neue Arbeitskleidung einkaufen gehen.

He can go shopping for some new work clothes.

Tatsächlich, das ist keine schlechte Idee.

Actually, that isn't a bad idea.

Dann hat er eine weitere Idee. Er ruft Sarah an.

Then he has another idea. He phones Sarah.

„Hast du bereits zu Mittag gegessen?" fragt er sie, als sie das Handy abhebt.

"Have you had lunch yet?" he asks her as she answers the phone.

„Noch nicht. Ich esse in einer halben Stunde zu Mittag, " antwortet sie.

"Not yet. I take my lunch in about half an hour," she replies.

„Fantastisch. Lass uns dann zusammen Mittag machen, " sagt Peter zu ihr. „Ich komme in die Stadt, um neue Kleidung zu kaufen. Wir haben ein schnelles Mittagessen zusammen, da morgen meine Ferien vorbei sind."

"Fantastic. Let's have lunch together then," Peter says to her. "I'm coming to town to buy some new clothes. We can have a quiet lunch together as my holiday is nearly over."

„Das wäre schön", antwortet Sarah freudig. „Ich werde dich beim italienischen Restaurant, an der Ecke von High Street treffen. Ich freue mich sehr darauf!"

"That would be lovely," Sarah replies, positively. "I will meet you at the Italian restaurant on the corner of the High Street. I am really looking forward to it!"

Peter ist ebenfalls sehr erfreut und rennt nach oben, um sich umzuziehen.

Peter is very pleased and runs upstairs to get changed.

Difficult Words

1- Felder – Fields

2- Legt sich hin – Lies down

3- Schlafen – Sleep

4- Nachmittag – Afternoon

5- Zusehen – To watch

6- Wann immer er möchte – Whenever he wants to

7- Er ruft an – He phones

8- Halb – Half

9- Ruhig – Quiet

10-Oben – Upstairs

11- Badezimmer – Bad

12-Auto – Car

13-Er mag nicht – He doesn't like

14-Heute – Today

15-Acht – Eight

Zusammenfassung der Geschichte:

Während Henry im Sommercamp beschäftigt ist, denkt Peter darüber nach, was er an seinem letzten Ferientag machen möchte. Er kehrt am nächsten Tag zur Arbeit zurück. Er denkt über verschiedene Möglichkeiten nach, bevor er sich für eine entscheidet.

Summary of the Story:

While Henry is busy at the summer camp, Peter thinks about what he wants to do on his last day of vacation since he goes back to work the next day. He considers several options before choosing one.

Quiz:

1) Warum möchte er nicht den Lebensmitteleinkauf für die nächste Woche machen?

a) Er mag Lebensmittel nicht allein einkaufen.

b) Er möchte nicht in die Stadt zurückkehren.

c) Er kann diese im Internet einkaufen, wann immer er möchte.

Why doesn't he want to go grocery shopping for next week?

a) Because he doesn't like to do the grocery alone.

b) Because he doesn't want to go back in town.

c) Because he can shop online whenever he wants to.

2) Warum ruft er Sarah an?

a) Um zu fragen, ob sie bereits zu Mittag gegessen hat.

b) Um zu fragen, ob sie sich besser fühlt.

c) Um sie zu fragen, was er mit dem Tag anfangen soll.

Why is he calling Sarah?

a) To ask if she had lunch already.

b) To ask if she feel better.

c) To ask an advice on what he should do of his day.

3) Welches Restaurant schlägt Sarah vor?

a) Ein italienisches Restaurant

b) Ein chinesisches Restaurant

c) Ein vietnamesisches Restaurant

What kind of restaurant does Sarah suggest?

a) An Italian restaurant

b) A Chinese restaurant

c) A Vietnamese restaurant

ANSWERS:

1) C

2) A

3) A

Peter und Henry haben am letzten Tag der Ferien Frühstück zusammen. Sarah ging früh zur Arbeit.

Peter and Henry are having breakfast together on the last day of the holidays. Sarah has gone to work early.

„Henry, heute müssen wir alle Hausarbeiten machen, so dass wir das Haus sauber und ordentlich zurück lassen, wenn wir nächste Woche zur Schule zurück gehen", sagt Peter.

"Henry, today, we need to do all the household jobs so that we leave the house clean and tidy when we go back to school next week," says Peter.

Henry lächelt und sagt, „Ich weiß, Papa. Ich weiß, wir haben heute einige harte Arbeiten zu machen. Können wir danach auch etwas backen?"

Henry smiles and says, "I know, Dad. I know we have to do some hard work today. Can we do some baking afterwards though?"

Peter stimmt einem Back-Nachmittag zu, nachdem sie alle ihre Arbeiten erledigt haben.

Peter agrees to a baking afternoon when they have finished doing all their jobs.

Henry bietet an, das Auto noch einmal zu reinigen – er hatte es genossen und machte es das letzte Mal gut.

Henry offers to clean the car again – he enjoyed that and did it well last time.

Peter sagt ihm, dass er zuerst sicher stellen soll, dass sein Bett ordentlich, seine Schultasche gepackt und seine Uniform bereit ist.

Peter tells him that first, he has to make sure that his bedroom is tidy, his school bag is packed, and his uniform is ready.

Henry ist nicht glücklich darüber, sein Bett ordentlich zu machen und geht langsam nach oben.

Henry isn't happy at having to tidy his bedroom, and goes upstairs slowly.

Peter räumt das Geschirr in den Geschirrspüler, reinigt die Küche und wischt dann den Küchenboden auf. Jetzt ist die Küche mehr oder weniger fertig.

Peter puts the dishes in the dishwasher, cleans the kitchen, then mops the kitchen floor. Now, the kitchen is more or less done.

Dann geht Peter nach oben zu den Badezimmern, um dort mit dem Reinigen zu beginnen. Er mag es nicht, die Badezimmer zu reinigen.

Peter then walks upstairs to the bathrooms to start cleaning there. He doesn't like cleaning the bathrooms.

Als er das beendet, erinnert er sich daran, Wäsche in die Waschmaschine zu legen. Dann bezieht er die Betten neu.

When he finishes that, he remembers to put some washing in the washing machine. Then he changes the beds.

Peter sagt Henry, dass er nach draußen geht, um den Rasen zu mähen. Er findet ihn in seinem Schlafzimmer und sagt ihm, dass sein Schlafzimmer nun ordentlich aussieht, also kann er nach draußen gehen und nun das Auto reinigen.

Peter tells Henry that he's going outside to mow the lawn. He finds him in his bedroom and tells him that his bedroom is looking tidy so he can go and clean the car now.

Peter und Henry gehen zusammen nach unten. Peter mäht den Rasen und Henry reinigt das Auto.

Peter and Henry go downstairs together. Peter mows the lawn and Henry cleans the car.

Und wieder macht Henry eine sehr gute Arbeit und das Auto glänzt sehr, als er fertig ist.

Again, Henry does a very good job and the car is very shiny when he finishes.

Auch der Garten sieht gut aus, als Peter fertig ist.

The garden looks good when Peter finishes, as well.

Sie bemerken, dass es nun Zeit ist für das Mittagessen, also setzen sie sich zusammen im Garten hin und essen ein Sandwich.

They realise it's time for lunch now so they sit down together in the garden and eat a sandwich.

Sie reflektieren glücklich darüber, was sie am Morgen gemacht hatten und einigen sich darauf, dass sie am Nachmittag etwas backen werden.

They reflect happily on what they have done this morning, and agree that they are going to do some baking in the afternoon.

„Was sollen wir zuerst machen? Den Schokoladenkuchen oder die Scones?" fragt Peter

"Which shall we make first? The chocolate cake or the scones?" Peter asks Henry an Henry.

Henry denkt für einen Augenblick nach und sag, „Mama liebt Schokoladenkuchen, also lass uns die Scones zuerst machen. Der Kuchen wird wärmer sein, wenn Mama nach Hause kommt und sie wird es lieben!".

Henry thinks for a moment and says, "Mum loves chocolate cake so let's make the scones first. The cake will be warmer when Mum gets home and she will love it!".

Difficult Words

1- Früh – Early

2- Hart – Hard

3- Geschirr – Dishes

4- Der Boden – The floor

5- Mehr oder weniger – More or less

6- Getan – Done

7- Waschmaschine – Washing machine

8- Lieben – To love

9- Wärmer – Warmer

10-Glänzend – Shiny

11- Nach unten gehen – Go downstairs

12-Letztes Mal – Last time

13-Badezimmer – Bathrooms

14-Glücklich – Happily

15-Sieht gut aus – Looks good

Zusammenfassung der Geschichte:

Es ist letzter Ferientag, und Peter und Henry haben eine Menge zu tun, bevor sie wieder zur Schule und zur Arbeit gehen. Sie entscheiden zusammen, wer was machen wird und was sie als Belohnung machen werden.

Summary of the Story:

It's the last day of vacation and Peter and Henry have a lot of work to do before going back to school and work. They decide together who will do what and what activity they will do as a reward.

Quiz:

1) Was ist die erste Aufgabe, die Henry tun muss?

a) Das Auto waschen.

b) Das Badezimmer sauber machen.

c) Sein Zimmer reinigen.

What is the first task that Henry has to do?

a) Clean the car.

b) Clean the bathroom.

c) Clean his room.

2) Wie steht Henry zu der Idee, dass er an seinem letzten Ferientag Hausarbeit machen muss?

a) Er ist nicht glücklich.

b) Er lächelt und ist bereit hart zu arbeiten.

c) Er zeigt keine Emotion, da er keine Wahl hat, zur Hausarbeit beizutragen.

How does Henry react at the idea of having to do housework on their last day of vacation?

a) He is not happy.

b) He smiles and is ready to work hard.

c) He has no emotion because he has no choice to contribute in the housework chore.

3) Welche der folgenden Tätigkeiten macht Peter nicht?

a) Die Küche reinigen.

b) Das Auto waschen.

c) Die Bettlaken wechseln.

Which of the following task Peter does not do?

a) Clean the kitchen.

b) Clean the car.

c) Change the sheets.

ANSWERS:

1) C

2) B

3) B

CONCLUSION

You have just completed the 30 short stories in this book. Congratulations!

We hope that the collection of stories you have read will encourage you to continue learning German. Reading can be one of the best---and most enjoyable--activities you could do to develop your language skills. Hopefully, you were able to experience that with this book.

If fully consumed as we have intended, these German short stories would widen your German vocabulary and the audio would allow you to follow along to the words, expose you to correct German pronunciation, and help you practice your listening comprehension.

If you need more help with learning German, please visit www.mydailygerman.com.

Cheers and best of luck to you!

My Daily German Team

HOW TO DOWNLOAD THE AUDIO?

Please take note that the audio are in MP3 format and need to be accessed online. No worries though; it's quite easy! Simply follow the instructions below. It will teach you the steps on where and how to download this book's accompanying audio.

On your computer, smartphone, iphone/ipad or tablet, go to this link:

https://mydailygerman.com/download-german-stories-beginners-audio/

Do you have any problems downloading the audio? If you do, feel free to send an email to support@mydailygerman.com. We'll do our best to assist you, but we would greatly appreciate if you thoroughly review the instructions first.

Thank you,

My Daily German Team

ABOUT MY DAILY GERMAN

MyDailyGerman.com believes that German can be learned almost painlessly with the help of a learning habit. Through its website and the books and audiobooks that it offers, German language learners are treated to high quality materials that are designed to keep them motivated until they reach their language learning goals.

Keep learning German and enjoy the learning process with books and audio from My Daily German.

Printed in Great Britain
by Amazon

44773960R00079